I REALLY NEEDED THIS
TODAY

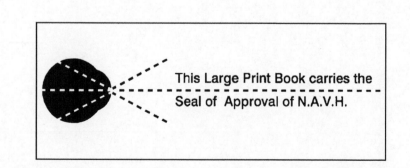

This Large Print Book carries the
Seal of Approval of N.A.V.H.

I REALLY NEEDED THIS TODAY

WORDS TO LIVE BY

HODA KOTB
WITH JANE LORENZINI

THORNDIKE PRESS
A part of Gale, a Cengage Company

GALE
A Cengage Company

Copyright © 2019 by To The Moon Entertainment, Inc.
Letter on pages 371–72 is reprinted courtesy of Ali Hazlett.
Thorndike Press, a part of Gale, a Cengage Company.

ALL RIGHTS RESERVED
Thorndike Press® Large Print Basic.
The text of this Large Print edition is unabridged.
Other aspects of the book may vary from the original edition.
Set in 16 pt. Plantin.

**LIBRARY OF CONGRESS CIP DATA ON FILE.
CATALOGUING IN PUBLICATION FOR THIS BOOK
IS AVAILABLE FROM THE LIBRARY OF CONGRESS**

ISBN-13: 978-1-4328-7688-3 (hardcover alk. paper)

Published in 2020 by arrangement with G. P. Putnam's Sons, an imprint
of Penguin Publishing Group, a division of Penguin Random House, LLC

Printed in Mexico
Print Number: 01   Print Year: 2020

If you've ever read a quote,
nodded your head, and thought,
I am not alone . . . this book
is for you.

INTRODUCTION

APHORISM noun *aph·o·rism*
the finest thoughts in the fewest words

That word! "Aphorism." Rhymes with . . . nothing. I'd never heard of it until I started doing some digging into why so many of us — including me — love inspirational quotes. Sociologist Murray Davis describes aphorisms as "the finest thoughts in the fewest words." Don't you just love that? I agree wholeheartedly. A great quote is just what you need, right when you need it, in the span of a hot second.

Davis says that aphorisms inspire us because they're both profound *and* universal. For example, "Absence makes the heart grow fonder." See? The quote nails a tender pang felt round the world in just six words.

I've always loved a meaningful quote, and I know so many of us do. They fill books and are celebrated on websites, T-shirts, cof-

7

fee mugs, calendars, and posters. (Remember the "Hang in There!" cat dangling from a branch?) Sometimes a quote reminds us of an old memory, reflects a hope, or maybe it hits home where we're sitting right now. If we laugh, all the better. Seemingly simple words tucked between quotation marks become the powerful elixir we need for so many reasons — to improve, renew, heal, guffaw, or just release. Ward Farnsworth, dean of the University of Texas School of Law, describes inspirational quotes as "little triumphs of rhetoric." I agree. They're like silent soldiers we carry with us into battle each day. After all, the unvarnished truth about the human condition is that being alive is both beautiful *and* painful, so we need ways to deal with that deep emotional arc. Quotes are both the bubbly and the balm to help us make it through our unpredictable journeys. Maybe quotes are the prayers we can't compose, the wings our spirits need to soar.

Have you ever sought out a quote? Searched for it as if your life depended on it, with tears of joy or sadness dripping onto the keyboard? Perhaps it's late into the night, or predawn, and the glow of your screen is acting as a lighthouse, beckoning those perfect words to safely navigate their way to your yearning head and heart. Quotes have saved so many of us — even for a moment — as life stitches its inevitable patterns of goodness and grief into the fabric of our lives. When my best friend's husband was in the fight of his life battling cancer, this quote jumped out at me: "God will, very likely, give you more than you can handle. He will not, however, give you more than He can handle." As I waited to find out if I'd ever be lucky enough to adopt a baby, these words, from Elizabeth Stone, bolstered my hope: "Making the decision to have a child — it is momentous. It is to decide forever to have your heart go walking around outside your body."

I can't imagine life without all of these B12 shots for the soul.

Almost daily, I'm pointing to a page or at a screen, saying to someone, "Look at this one!" Like *I* wrote the quote. There's something so fun about sharing one, and you want the person you're engaging with to laugh — or cry — right along with you. So many times I think, *Wow . . . that handful of words just changed my day.* One sentence and you're enlightened, and it doesn't cost one penny! On the days you feel happy and motivated, a quote can serve as a booster rocket, launching you even further into that

Good Day zone. If you wake up grumpy or lazy, a few well-crafted words can sell you on the idea that putting on a smile or a pair of running shoes might just be worth it.

Certain quotes stick with me from speeches I've watched. I remember one delivered by professional speaker Patricia Russell-McCloud. The crowd was totally with her as she talked about how we all carry burdens and have mountains to climb. She confirmed to nodding heads how challenging life can be, with a mountain always looming. And then, her quote: "You know what I say to that mountain? 'Mount-aaaaaaaain,' I say, 'get out of my way!' " Preach!

I'm a sucker for a good speech or song or quote that inspires and motivates me. I've always leaned in to people with goose-bump-raising stuff to share. After all, how many experiences are we going to have in our lives? Plenty. But we're never going to have them all, so I look for people who've gone through something I haven't. I get to feel what they felt and be moved by what moved them. It makes me feel alive, and even more prepared for challenges. "Get out of my way!"

We may just be wired to seek out a boost for our heart and soul. Media psychology expert and communications consultant Scott Sobel says that "inspirational quotes affect us on a primal level." Describing human nature as "aspirational," performance psychologist Jonathan Fader says quotes can be powerful in changing our thinking and helping us see something in ourselves that we want to change or overcome.

I suppose that's what drove me to post an inspirational quote on Instagram back in December 2013, when the app hadn't yet turned three. It was New Year's Eve, so the quote I chose, attributed to C. S. Lewis, reflected hope for a fresh start and positive year ahead: "There are far, far better things ahead than any we leave behind." To my surprise, nearly 2,900 people "liked" the quote. Wow! I thought I was just trying to encourage myself.

For the next month I continued to post quotes, but not regularly. By the time February rolled around — and more and more people were actively engaging — I had committed to several days of sharing quotes on my Insta page. The whole process easily became part of my morning routine, and there was (and still is) a safe feeling about Instagram, right? It's a kind space for the most part, and when you're there you feel like no one's out to get you. I also love the cozy format, the way the words and images nestle together inside the rounded square.

So now, when it comes to selecting a quote, here's how I do it. At around three forty-five a.m., I carve out fifteen minutes total to jot down what I'm grateful for in my yesterday, and then I'll poke around the web or Pinterest for a quote to post, one that holds meaning either for me or for someone on my mind. (Within this book, some quotes I chose are from well-known sources. Some are from my friends and family. Others are proverbs or phrases whose origins are seemingly impossible to track down! I did my best to attribute each quote, but some of the clues as to who said what are lost in time.)

Sometimes I don't even know what I need until I see a quote and I get emotional reading the words. It's almost like someone's holding my hand. *I'm with you. I'm going through it, too.* For me, the pick-me-up is knowing that someone else has felt or is feeling the exact same way I am — lost, lonely, forgotten, sad, or stuck. Sure, they're just words, but maybe they'll motivate me to get up and out of my funk. If I'm comforted only for the seconds I'm soaking up the quote, isn't that enough?

When followers on Instagram do more

than "like" a quote I've posted — when they comment — I find it very interesting to scroll through their responses. I'm always intrigued that the same quote — the very same words — sparks different reactions. It's as if everybody's nodding yes at the same time but for a wide range of reasons. Here's a particularly moving example of this "universal yet individual" phenomenon. I posted: "For all the things my hands have held the best by far is you." Soon, a whole bunch of moms commented about the joy of holding their babies, but one person described the beauty of holding her dying father's hand in hers. What a lovely and unexpected reminder about the many things we hold dear, and about the circle of life.

In so many ways, social media (like Instagram) connect us, but certainly technology can isolate us, too. Julianne Holt-Lunstad, a psychologist at Brigham Young University who's studied social isolation, says, "Technology has sanded away the necessity and inconvenience of interacting with other human beings: we can work from home, order groceries online, stream movies from bed. At the same time, the percentage of Americans who participate in social groups — whether they be social clubs, sports teams, community centers, volunteer organizations, or religious groups — has fallen."

While most of us (I hope) aren't chronically lonely, I'll bet we often feel alone with our pain or anxiety or fear. I know I do sometimes. That's why it's so comforting when a posted quote not only is received but is met with an outpouring of empathy. With one click of a button, you put something out into the ether and go about your day, and all of a sudden you read in the comment section: *That sounds like me* or *Mary, this made me think of us.* Wait a minute. On your saddest day, you post a quote because you're feeling alone, but what you don't anticipate is that *those* are the types of quotes that resonate most often with people. "Exactly how I'm feeling!" We think we're sitting alone with our private pain, but the truth is, hurt and heartache connect us all, as do love and laughter and hope.

I think that's why this book feels so right to me, especially now. There's a significant need for things that bring us together instead of pulling us apart. This book is for everybody. I don't care where you live, where you're from, what walk of life you're in — it doesn't matter. Herein are words that have stood the test of time, as well as others that address our now and our next.

They're meant to teach, inspire, entertain, and soothe us. Couldn't we all use a reminder that there are so many more things we have in common than things that make us different? *I feel that, he feels that, she feels that, we all feel it.*

In my mind, this is a book meant not only to be read but to be used. I picture you sipping a cup of hot coffee, cracking open the book, and reading it in bite-sized pieces. One at a time, one for the day, see if it speaks to you. I've added my own thoughts about what the quotes mean to me or how they relate to moments and people in my life.

In the year ahead, may you find the perfect way to read and use this book in your daily life. And if the experience is meaningful to you, I hope you'll consider sharing it with someone else, someone who might just say — right along with you — *"I really needed this today."*

JANUARY 1

What the new year brings to you will
depend a great deal on what you bring to
the new year.
— VERN MCLELLAN

I'll never forget what the year 2007 brought
me: Kathie Lee Gifford. We met by hap-
penstance at a restaurant in New York City,
she agreed to fill in on the fourth hour of
Today, and what followed was an eleven-
year professional and personal relationship I
truly treasure. One of the *Today* producers
still likes to joke with me that I was "just
wandering the halls of NBC" until she came
up with the idea to invite Kathie Lee to co-
host on the fourth hour. Pretty close to true.
Kathie Lee absolutely set me on a path I'd
never imagined for myself. I'm still amazed
— and grateful — that meeting just one
person can change your day, your year, your
life. Thanks, Kath, and cheers to a new year!

Your wings already exist. All you have to
do is fly.

I think we're born with wings. It just takes a
while to test them, like when we first jump
off a swing or pedal like crazy when a parent lets go of the bike. I just knew I was
soaring when my dad launched me into the
air from the pool, my little foot blasting up
from his laced fingers. Try not to forget
we've had wings since forever.

January 5

I am better off healed than I ever was
unbroken.

— Beth Moore

After I had surgery to remove cancer in my
breast, a kind nurse gently cleaned around
my wounds as I stood in front of a mirror.
There we were . . . me, her, and my broken
reflection. *Who in the world is ever going to
want to see this or be near it?* I was overwhelmed with fear and insecurity. Fast-
forward to now, when, thankfully, I have a
man in my life who loves me beyond and
for my scars. Scars mean we've healed, that
we've grown stronger. They are the very
thing that cuts through the BS regarding
what matters in life and who we want to
share it with. Don't you think it's our scars
that connect us?

JANUARY 6

Be careful who you pretend to be. You might forget who you are.

I think as we get older there's less pretending. Year after year, our internal blueprints develop into a solid structure where we move about the world as ourselves. Still, I like this message — a reminder to keep it real.

JANUARY 7

Do not judge. You don't know what storm
I've asked her to walk through.

— God

On the twentieth anniversary of the mass
shooting at Columbine High School, I
interviewed both survivors and people who
had lost family members that horrific day. I
was absolutely blown away by the strength
of spirit and love in the room. One mother,
Beth Nimmo, lost her seventeen-year-old
daughter, Rachel, but vowed to go one step
further beyond just forgiving the gunmen
for killing her daughter — she met with one
of the shooters' mother. "We both lost our
children, but she had all the shame, the
reproach," Beth said, "and the hate." Before
the meeting, Beth asked God what to say to
Sue Klebold when they sat before each
other. "The Lord said, ask her who her son
was before April 20, 1999." When the

women met, Beth said her question touched Sue, who began crying. "She said, 'Nobody wants to know anything about my little boy that I raised,' " Beth recalled, through tears of her own. "I saw a mother's heart."

So, if you are too tired to speak, sit next to me, because I, too, am fluent in silence.

— R. Arnold

When my father died suddenly when I was in college, I walked around in a fog. I deliberately didn't wear my glasses so everything remained out of focus; my earplugs stayed in, blaring music. One day in class, as a test was under way, I just snapped. *I can't do this. I'm outta here.* I got up and grabbed my backpack. On my way out the door, the professor said, "If you don't take this test, you're going to fail." I couldn't have cared less. My friend Peggy Fox, who was also taking the test, picked up her backpack and followed me out. When we sat down at a picnic table by the duck pond, Peggy didn't say a word. Her mere presence was enough to comfort a small piece of my broken heart.

JANUARY 9

When you look into your mother's eyes,
you know that is the purest love you can
find on this earth.

— MITCH ALBOM

For the last eleven years and counting, I've called my mom each day at 11:01 a.m., right after the fourth hour of *Today* when I get off the set. Every time, she sounds like it's the first day she's seen me do the show. "Oh, you were amazing!" she'll say. "I just saw you and I cannot believe the purple dress!" Or, "Oh, Hodie, I can't believe it! How do you seem so rested?" Now, usually you get the parental pom-poms in spurts . . . but *not* with her. They're always shaking. After I adopted Hope, it wasn't long before my mom started to ask me when I was getting off maternity leave. She missed seeing me every morning! When I popped back for one day during my time off to watch the

Thomas Rhett concert in Rockefeller Plaza, she taped the show and texted me the clip. "Amaaazzzing!" she wrote with lots of *a*'s and *z*'s. C'mon! Only now, with daughters, do I have some idea about how my mom feels about my siblings — Hala and Adel — and me. My entire perspective on that depth of love has changed forever.

If you ever get caught sleeping at work, just slowly raise your head and say, "In Jesus's name I pray."

I'm not promoting this, but I am laughing out loud at it.

JANUARY 11

Never be defined by your past. It was just
a lesson, not a life sentence.

This is such a refreshing perspective on the
past. It really shouldn't be a ball and chain
we lug around, should it? Maybe there's
something we can redefine today to feel
more free.

JANUARY 12

Actually, you are good enough.

Tell yourself. Tell someone else.
Spread the word.

JANUARY 13

The elimination diet: Remove anger, re-
gret, resentment, guilt, blame, and worry.
Then watch your health, and life, improve.
— Charles F. Glassman

Just like sugar and salt, some of that emotional stuff can be addictive, can't it? When
we think about our New Year's resolutions,
maybe we should add cutting back on the
negative self-talk, too.

JANUARY 14

Hardships often prepare ordinary people for an extraordinary destiny.
— *Voyage of the Dawn Treader*

So true. I think when we fight through challenges, Destiny — in her own time — takes notice. *Okay . . . I see that muscle of yours. I've got something special planned for you.*

Talk about your blessings more than you
talk about your problems.

I agree, it's almost always best to focus on
what's going right in your life — except on
a girls' trip. In a hotel room or on a beach
somewhere, girls are gonna wear out their
problems until the Doritos and dip are
gone. Then, after a grocery run, they're
gonna rehash the same problems while
laughing their heads off, so . . .

There are moments in life when you miss someone so much that you just want to pick them from your dreams and hug them for real.

I wish, Dad.

A junior in college, I'd never really had anything go wrong in my life. But one night, at Virginia Tech, everything changed . . . forever. Out of the blue, my brother, Adel, showed up at my sorority formals to tell me that my dad had died from a heart attack. My world went black. I'd suddenly lost the most important man in my life. Nothing made sense. At fifty-one, my dad had recently been told by doctors he had the heart of a thirty-one-year-old. Now all of our hearts were broken. So many years later, the pain of missing my father is still potent, especially now with his granddaughters in my arms. I've begun to bring up my dad during our "night night" routine with Haley: "G'night, Teta, g'night, Mommy and Daddy." Then we look up at the ceiling and say, "G'night, God." And next, hearing that little voice say my dad's name moves me for so many different reasons: "G'night, Abdel." Good night, Dad.

Put your hair up in a bun, drink some coffee, and handle it.

Totally agree with the order of events here.
You ready?

I think one of my favorite feelings is laughing with someone and realizing halfway through how much you enjoy them and their existence.

I won't say who (rhymes with "Kathy Ryan"), but someone made me laugh so hard I wet my pants. During my show on Sirius radio, my dear friend and assistant Kathy started to pretend she was supportive of my new purse, one with lots of little compartments. Anyone who knows me well — and Kathy does — knows I am *the* most unorganized person when it comes to stuff. My purse is more like a clown car, with cords and glasses and receipts flowing from it in an endless stream of chaos. So, when I showed Kathy my new "system," she started in on me: "Oh, look! I'll put my coins in here and all of my chargers will fit in this pocket quite nicely. Well, look here! Perfect for all of my pens!" (She's rolling her eyes the whole time.) "I'll know where everything is at all times." I was laughing so hard I couldn't speak. Of course, she was right. I don't have the purse anymore, but I will *always* have Kathy in my life. She's one of the funniest people I know . . . and love.

JANUARY 19

One of the best feelings in the world is knowing your presence and absence both mean something to someone.

I'm still astounded when two little someones cry when I leave the room. And they practically throw me a parade when I come back home. Haley and Hope, you are my some-ones.

JANUARY 20

Being deeply loved by someone gives you strength, while loving someone deeply gives you courage.

— Lao Tzu

Send some love out into the world today, even if it's just across the kitchen table.

Last night, sitting on the couch with my
   husband,
I said, "I love you."
He asked, "Is that you or the wine
   talking?"
I said, "It's me . . . talking to the wine."

I love Carson Daly's comment about this
post: *My mom would framethis!*

When I first met Carson at NBC, I only
knew him as the MTV music guy . . . the
guy who was really funny and a great host.
But as I started working more often with
Carson, I saw a deeper side to him, especially in 2017, when he lost both parents
within a span of five weeks. His father's
health had been up and down for some
time, but his mother's death was a shock.
After some time off, he joined me on set
and shared his grief: "It's hard to grasp

January 23

Be here now.

— Ram Dass

In the twelve years since I've known my friend Jennifer Miller, she's probably said these very words to me a few dozen times. It's a phrase she learned from her mother, Bev, whom I never had the honor of meeting. "Be here now." Her mom's words serve as a memory for Jen and a mantra for us all — a suggestion, a reminder, a verbal tap on the shoulder. Whenever Jen says it to me it's because she wants to honor our little sliver of now, whatever and wherever that may be. "Wow — look around, Hoda. We get to be here now."

JANUARY 24

By being yourself, you put something wonderful in the world that was not there before.

— Edwin Elliot

Celebrate your special today! Remember: you are you-nique.

January 25

You may have to fight a battle more than once to win it.

— Margaret Thatcher

If you feel battle weary today, I hope this one is a boost. We might be worn out, but we're all in for the win — eventually!

January 26

All of it is a mind-set. All of it is about being consistent and doing the right things. Honestly, we all have the capacity. We all have in us the ability to do whatever it is that we want to do and just work hard.
— Jennifer Lopez

I've met a lot of hard workers, and Jennifer Lopez is at the top of that list. I've interviewed her before the start of several tours and each time was amazed watching her prepare. Jennifer rehearses a routine until it's perfect, and then she rehearses a little bit more. J. Lo *defines* hard worker.

Every good thing that has happened in
your life happened because something
changed.
— ANDY ANDREWS

A job, an address, a season, an outlook, and
(of course) underwear. Anything changing
for you today?

JANUARY 28

Wake up, beauty. It's time to beast.

Let's tackle this day in beast mode!

You only live once? False. You live every day. You only die once.

What I loved most about chef Leah Chase was that she hugged you like your mom would hug you. She did that to me and to everyone she fed at her beloved New Orleans restaurant, Dooky Chase. Known as the Queen of Creole Cuisine, Leah brought people together with her amazing food for a whopping seventy-five years and won the James Beard Foundation's Lifetime Achievement Award at age ninety-three. Can't you just feel her passion? "I tell people all the time, you have to be in love with that pot. You have to put all of your love into that pot. If you're in a hurry, just eat your sandwich and go. Don't even start cooking, because you can't do anything well in a hurry." In 2019, Leah passed away at age ninety-six. I'll miss her food, but mostly, I'll miss those awesome hugs.

JANUARY 30

Life will get better if you let it.

— Gary Trainor

Meghan Trainor choked up a bit sharing this quote with me. The words are her father's. "He's my guy. He's the one," she says. "Everything I do, I'm inspired by him." Her dad has spoken those words throughout her life, comforting and encouraging her whenever she complains about something. The singer-songwriter says the phrase is a reminder that while so much of her journey is beyond her control, what she *can* affect is her attitude. A positive outlook — no matter what happens — is within her reach.

January 31

God gave us mouths that close and ears
that don't . . . that should tell us
something.

Until I met Kathie Lee I wasn't listening
well during my interviews at *Dateline* NBC.
Instead, I was thinking, *What's my next
question? How am I going to approach this?
What do I need for the story?* Frankly, I
didn't focus fully on the answer that was
unfolding right in front of me. All of that
changed when Kathie Lee called me out on
set one day and said, "Would you just get
rid of those darn cards? Just *toss* them!"
Huh? Get rid of the show topic cards so
carefully prepared for us by our producers?
That didn't seem smart. But I did it. I
tossed them into the air and began a journey
of loosening my news corset and living in
the moment. It worked well for me during
the fourth hour of *Today* and for *Dateline,*

too. From that point on I didn't refer so much to my lists of questions and even tucked the cards under my leg sometimes during interviews. I can't believe how far into my career it took me to learn that, but at least I did.

FEBRUARY 1

You have brains in your head. You have feet in your shoes. You can steer yourself any direction you choose.

— Dr. Seuss

Correct from head to toe!

FEBRUARY 2

Trust the wait. Embrace the uncertainty. Enjoy the beauty of becoming. When nothing is certain, anything is possible.

— Mandy Hale

As laid-back as I am about most stuff, I've also got some control freak in me. I suppose I've gotten better at embracing the uncertainty over the years because so many things have happened in my life that I never imagined — from breast cancer, to divorce, to adopting children. At some point you realize that no matter how much you want to drive, sometimes you're better off in the backseat enjoying the view. I think the tricky part is recognizing when to take charge and when to take a nap and let everything take care of itself.

FEBRUARY 3

Never assume that loud is strong and quiet is weak.

This reminds me of Adel, my gentle — and strong — brother. There are a million examples of his constant quiet strength, but I'll simply share this. I cannot imagine what it was like for Adel, one February night during our time together at Virginia Tech, to walk into my sorority formal and ask me to go outside with him. Calmly, he watched my smiling face turn to worry as I noted his street clothes. What was going on? At first I thought he'd crashed our formal, but then I was just confused. "Just come outside with me," he said, shuffling me out, gently settling me inside a car as I begged him to tell me what was happening. Those steps, those moments leading up to his telling me that our father had died suddenly, must have been excruciating, even as he was managing his own shock and grief. The millions of examples? They don't matter. That's all you need to know about my brother, Adel.

February 4

Accept what people offer.
Drink their milkshakes.
Take their love.

— Wally Lamb

Why is it so hard sometimes to simply take things we're offered? And why is it so hard to ask for help? I've never been great at it. In fact, there's that exercise where you pretend to ask your former partners why the relationship ended. Is there a common reason? I think the answer about me would be: "She didn't need me enough." I'm still a work in progress on this, but with Joel, I'm trying to do better. He's so good at offering, too. "Let me get this. I've got this. I'll take care of it." Now, instead of saying, "No, that's okay," I try to say more often, "How nice. Thank you." (Especially if it's a milkshake.)

February 5

Speak your mind — even if your voice shakes.

— Maggie Kuhn

I posted this after a dear friend found the courage to tell me that I wasn't providing the support she needed during a deeply difficult time in her life. I could tell in her lead-up to actually sharing those words that the process was agonizing. Ultimately, our interchange was beautifully real . . . and she was right. I thanked her for calling me out, with her voice shaking.

FEBRUARY 6

I'm nicer when I like my outfit.

Sure, I love to feel good in what I'm wearing. Who doesn't? But I'm just not that in tune when it comes to how often I'm wearing my favorites. In fact, I tend to *over*-wear them. When I first started on the fourth hour of *Today,* producers jokingly showcased how clothes-blind I am by airing a series of video clips and photos of me wearing the same orange sweater. I loved that sweater! It became known as the "lucky sweater," a kind way of saying, "Get rid of that thing!" What can I say? I love hard.

FEBRUARY 7

Ask what makes you come alive, and go
do it.
— HOWARD THURMAN

My friend and *Today* colleague Maria
Shriver has a great way of taking the heat
off a momentous question we sometimes
ask ourselves: what's my purpose? Yikes.
Cue the anxiety and self-doubt, right?
Instead, Maria poses this question: what do
I find meaningful? The answer to that, she
says, will lead you to where you're supposed
to be. I like that. What in the course of your
day brings you meaning? Helping someone?
Going to church? Maybe if we try changing
the question — reframing it — we'll inch
closer to what makes us feel most alive.

FEBRUARY 8

Cupcakes are muffins that believed in miracles.

Believe, every day. The frosting is coming . . . sprinkles too!

FEBRUARY 9

You have been assigned this mountain so that you can show others it can be moved.
— Mel Robbins

I love this quote because it not only offers a reason *why* we were handed a crap sandwich, it provides motivation and purpose: "Hey, if you get through this, others will believe that they can, too."

FEBRUARY 10

Behind all your stories is always your
mother's story, because hers is where
yours begins.

— Mitch Albom

My mother's story can't be told without using the words "strength" and "optimism."
Throughout my life, I've watched her wake
up determined and happy, no matter what.
Growing up, we three kids were awakened
by her cheery voice and the Arabic word for
"big sunrise" or "great big sun" . . . something like that. Everything was sunny in our
world. Even when she lost her husband with
two kids in college and one newly graduated, Mom was strong and hopeful and
there for us. Because of her, I got to soak
up such a winning combination of powerful
qualities. Now when I open the blinds in
my apartment, Haley says, "Good morning,
New York! Good morning, Hudson River!"

I love that. My mom taught me to be optimistic at sunrise and now I can do the same for my daughter. I think it's the best thing you can give your kid — thinking that no matter what, the world is good.

FEBRUARY 11

One day or day one. You decide.
— Paulo Coelho

One day is the day you forget, right? *Day one* is the day you never forget. Day one you start a new job, you quit an old job, you say, "I do." It's the beginning. Choose day one!

FEBRUARY 12

Your mind knows only some things. Your inner voice, your inner instinct knows everything. If you listen to what you know instinctively, it will always lead you down the right path.

— Henry Winkler

For so many years, I think my heartbeat was also a-tap-tap-tapping on my soul. *You can be a mom. It's not too late.* I truly believe that when I finally found the courage to say what I wanted out loud, fate began to work its magic. If there's something you're yearning for, perhaps consider giving it a voice, even if you start with a whisper.

FEBRUARY 13

The struggle you're facing is a test to see if you're truly committed to the life you say you want.

Life has a way of testing us, doesn't it? My parents prepared my sister, brother, and me for that reality not only by raising us to work hard but by showing us what that looked like. I was so proud of my dad when he left his steady government job and started his own company, International Petroleum Consulting Service, right on Pennsylvania Avenue in Washington, DC. My mother's career and social circle were built within the shelves of the Library of Congress, a journey that spanned more than thirty years. I hope to raise my kids with the same drive, enough to truly commit to the life they want to live.

FEBRUARY 14

We are most alive when we're in love.
— John Updike

There's a lot to love about Valentine's Day,
but plenty of happy February fourteenths
have passed me by, just like a gorgeous
bouquet headed for someone else's desk.
Honestly, I can remember *hating* Valentine's
Day. My pat answer was "Nope, no plans
for V-Day." Many V-Days passed without
cards or flowers. Plus, I met my ex-husband
on Valentine's Day and my divorce papers
arrived in the mail on Valentine's Day. After
I shared that double whammy with Kathie
Lee one Valentine's Day in the makeup
room, we walked onto our passion-packed
set, complete with roses and red balloons. I
started off the show with a "Happy Valentine's!" greeting, to which Kathie Lee
replied, "Not for you!" I had to come clean
on the air. So, if this day is a rough one for

you . . . I get it.

For everyone in love — we're very happy for you. But, if you're having a crap day because you're not, we are holding your hand.

February 15

There's power in looking silly and not caring that you do.
— AMY POEHLER

I've always found that children create this space for us, and maybe that's why I love them so much. When you're with kids, before you know it you're wearing a chef's hat with stickers all over your face, shaking maracas, and singing a silly song about pickles. The *best*!

February 16

It will never be perfect. Make it work.

— Life

Well, fine. Watch me.

73

It is amazing what you can accomplish if you do not care who gets the credit.
— Harry S. Truman

Let me just say this. Rope, Anthony, Tommy, and Jimmy — you guys are the best. These aren't just the guys behind the cameras at NBC, they're the guys I see when I come into work at four fifteen a.m. — who've been there for hours — who high-five me with a smile. They ask how the baby slept. They're the guys who wonder when my mom's coming again with a batch of baklava. I know you've got people in your work or home life who do the teamwork to make the dream work. Tell 'em you love 'em today!

February 18

Being sisters means you always have backup.

My sister, Hala, has always had my back. After I was diagnosed with breast cancer, I had to undergo an MRI so doctors could determine exactly where the disease was lurking. Maybe some people don't bat an eye in an MRI tube, but I'm not one of them. Can't stand it. When the technician warned Hala and me that due to radioactivity, I had to go alone into the MRI room, Hala walked in anyway. She pulled over a chair and sat next to me. "There can't be anyone else in the room," the tech said again. Hala wasn't having it. "Nope. Start the machine," she said. "I'm staying right here." That's just one of endless examples of Hala's serving as my backup. That Haley and Hope will see this — and learn it — means everything.

Be you, bravely.

And let's double down on brave with this: "Be yourself. Everyone else is already taken."

FEBRUARY 20

When a flower doesn't bloom, you fix the environment in which it grows, not the flower.

— Alexander den Heijer

Right? Maybe it's a job that isn't the right fit. Maybe it's a relationship that's dragging us down. We so often think the problem is us, but — *argh* — we'd save so much time if we realized it's actually the toxic soil where we've set down roots.

God does not always take us where we
want to go, but He always leads us where
we need to be.

— Martha Finley

I noticed the other day that page after page
in my journals is filled with prayers. "God,
please . . ." on days I was asking for help.
"God, thank you . . ." on so many days.
Flipping through and seeing that was a good
reminder of how much faith plays a role in
my daily life, whether I'm on my knees or
on the mountaintop.

FEBRUARY 22

Everything will be okay.

It's not always easy to believe this, but it's *always* nice to hear it. Moments before I went into the operating room to have cancer removed from my breast, my mom was standing next to the bed, terrified. I remember watching as my incredibly kind and skilled surgeon, Dr. Freya Schnabel, moved toward my mom. She looked into her eyes and said, "I'm going to take good care of your little girl." I can still picture my mom's face . . . relief just washed over it. Freya had made a promise to us both in that moment, one that she kept.

FEBRUARY 23

Your first thought in the morning should be "Thank you."

You can choose whatever you want for your second one!

FEBRUARY 24

There's only one thing more precious than
our time and that's who we spend it on.
— Leo Christopher

We're pulled in so many directions every
day! We watch the clock, eager to get back
to our most precious connections. Missing
people is hard, but aren't we lucky to have
such special souls in our lives?

FEBRUARY 25

We don't hide the crazy, we parade it down the street.

The first year I covered Mardi Gras for WWL-TV in New Orleans, producers asked me what I'd decided on for my costume. *Huh? We're wearing costumes on air? Well, okay.* I chose a devil costume and took the screwdriver they handed me — the kind you drink. Cheers! There I was, dressed up with the rest of the news team. It was wild. The hard-core investigative reporter had on a clown nose. The buttoned-up reporter who covered nothing but politics was now a crawfish. Everybody was in, and I loved it. I learned quickly that the attitude during Mardi Gras is: if you don't dress up, we know who you are. There are *so* many things I love about that city, but one of my favorites is how New Orleans gets its crazy on during the week of Mardi Gras.

February 26

The word "listen" contains the same letters as the word "silent."

— Alfred Brendel

I'm guilty of this one . . . not always listening. Instead, if a family member or friend shares a concern, I start dialing or scrolling for ideas, trying to fix the problem. Sometimes I think it's better to just sit with someone and let them vent. Then continue to zip it . . . and see if there's anything more they need to get off their chest.

Sometimes I just look up, smile, and say,
"I know that was you. Thank you."

I love meeting people in Rockefeller Plaza whenever our *Today* segments move us outside. It's my favorite part of the show! One morning, I spotted a particular sign in a sea of many, all creative and fun. A woman was holding a white poster that read: "Hoda, ask me about my bracelet." Off air, I went over to her and started chatting. She explained that she used to work as my father's secretary at West Virginia University, where he taught engineering. Calling him a "very kind man," she showed me a silver bracelet he brought back for her after a trip to Egypt. Of course he did . . . my very kind dad. My heart swelled with pride and I missed him. When she so generously offered me the bracelet, I took it, certain my dad was with us that day on the plaza.

FEBRUARY 28

Always be a little kinder than necessary.
— James M. Barrie

One evening, I was headed up to my apartment, sharing the elevator with a young woman I'd never seen before. Petite and wearing a green knit beanie topped with two eye stalks, the girl was staring at her feet as we glided upward. When I commented on the heavenly aroma wafting from her tray of cupcakes, she told me they were salted caramel. And then she exited. The next day, a small box awaited me at my apartment building's front desk. Atop was a handwritten note:

"You were admiring my cupcakes last night in the elevator (Oscar the Grouch hat) and unfortunately they were all spoken for or I would have offered you one. I had a bit of extra time in my schedule today, so I picked up a sample for you. Enjoy! Lisa."

What?! I couldn't believe what a stranger had done for me. She chose to spend her "extra time" doing something so thoughtful for me. I'll always remember you, Lisa, and your reminder that small gestures can make a big — and beautiful — difference.

If your actions create a legacy that inspires others to dream more, learn more, do more, and become more, then, you are an excellent leader.

— Dolly Parton

This makes me think of teachers. One of my favorites as a child was Mrs. Rosebrock, my ninth-grade teacher. I'll never forget the very first day I walked into her classroom. "Sharing the Night Together" by Dr. Hook was blasting from a cassette player. Wow! A teacher — an adult — was welcoming us with *our* music. Throughout the year, she encouraged us students to think creatively and be ourselves. With my octagon-shaped glasses and funny name, I felt so grateful to Mrs. Rosebrock for making me feel like fitting in was possible . . . and for teaching me how.

MARCH 1

Sometimes you just have to be done. Not mad, not upset. Just done.

We've all had one . . . a toxic person in our life who's always on the make and the take. One day, you're just over them. You decide — that's it. No drama . . . you just go out like a lamb, not a lion. It's called freedom.

MARCH 2

Character is how you treat those who can do nothing for you.

I think a character check is one of the quickest ways to figure out if a second date is in order. Restaurants are the best for this. I remember being so turned off and upset by a date who not only sent back his meal but was dismissive to the server. Extra yucky. Buh-bye.

MARCH 3

Recipe for iced coffee:

1. Have kids.
2. Make coffee.
3. Forget you made coffee.
4. Drink it cold.

If you even remember your coffee cup is in the microwave from the last time you attempted to reheat it.

March 4

It's a good day to have a good day.

The other day at the gym, I saw a woman trying to race out, late for something. She said she was a schoolteacher and that she'd just called her kids to wake them up, plus she had a field trip to get to. "Oh my God, I've forgotten my bra and my shirt." Ahhhh! That's the worst feeling, isn't it? No bra, no shirt, no service. But here's what she did. I watched her take control back. She pulled out a sweater from her gym bag, put it on, and wrapped a belt around the whole deal. "It is going to be a good day," she said with a smile. Everything was unraveling but she wasn't having it. "It's beautiful outside and I'm saying thank you, God, for today." I won't ever forget her and that masterful reset. It *is* a good day to have a good day, isn't it?

MARCH 5

Peace comes when our hearts are open
like the sky, vast as the ocean.
— JACK KORNFIELD

When my family and I roll into Rehoboth
Beach, we have a few pit stops that never
change. First, the Coffee Mill, an awesome
hangout. We drink coffee with Anne — a
longtime regular — and soak up the fresh,
salty air. After a catch-up with owners Mel
and Bob, we head to the beach for the day.
By noon, there's no conversation about
where we're eating. Lunch is *always* at Go
Fish!, because Alison serves up the best fish
and chips you've ever had. Then, back to
the beach, dinner in, and a full night's sleep
that only the beach can induce. I'll bet you
have a place just like this. A place where —
when you Google it — a red pin appears
with the word "peace" written next to it.

God doesn't give us the people we want.
He gives us the people we need. To love
us, to hurt us, to leave us, to help us, and
to make us into the person that we are
today.

— Melaney Mendez

I'm so glad someone else is in charge of all
this. Thanks, God.

MARCH 7

Because when you stop and look around,
this life is pretty amazing.
— Dr. Seuss

I usually get this feeling when I'm running
in Central Park. No matter what's on my
mind or in my heart, there's something so
inspiring when I look up into the trees and
across the water. Everyone around me is active and the scenery keeps changing. New
York City has a way of making you feel
small because it's so vast, but in the park, I
feel connected to everyone and everything.
I hope you find time to soak up one of your
favorite places today.

MARCH 8

Don't wait for someone to bring you flowers. Plant your own garden and decorate your own soul.

— Mario Quintana

I do think you have to make your own magic sometimes. When I worked in Fort Myers, Florida, I drove to Key Largo looking for . . . something. At that very first key, I checked into a hotel and then went outside to walk around. After a while, around midnight, someone yelled to me: "C'mon! Get on board and go fishing with us!" Hmm. There was a big moon and there was that "something," so I hopped aboard. What a magical night! We caught fish and drank beer, and when we got back to shore, someone grilled the catch and it was delicious. I'd never have guessed all of that would happen when I rolled into Key Largo, and I won't soon forget that night.

What a great reminder to at least crack open the door so something awesome can walk through it.

March 9

It's not how much we give but how much love we put into giving.
> — Saint Teresa of Calcutta

What comes to mind is a homemade pencil holder sitting on a teacher's desk, the elbow macaroni lovingly glued to a hand-painted tin can. Or the amazing pink blanket a woman I don't even know knitted for Hope. It's easy to feel overwhelmed by what it means to be charitable, but really, it's the small gestures with big love behind them that matter so much. Any little thing you can do for someone today?

March 10

So many people love you. Don't focus on those who don't.

Why do we do that? Same story when — in a sea of positive posts on social media — we fixate on the *one* negative comment. The awesome author and speaker Brené Brown says something I love: "Don't grab that hurtful stuff from the cheap seats and pull it close . . . Just let it fall to the ground . . . You just gotta step over it and keep going." The concept of moving on is powerful. At least when you put yourself out there, you're trying to make a difference or be real. Maybe focus today on all the people who are in your front row.

MARCH 11

If you want to be happy, you have to be happy on purpose. When you wake up, you can't just wait to see what kind of day you'll have. You have to decide what kind of day you'll have.

— Joel Osteen

I love that phrase, "happy on purpose." It's rooted in a concept that I really believe in: happiness is a choice. Maybe you don't feel like trying today, but perhaps give it a go. You may just make your own day!

March 12

A lot of beautiful things can happen if only you believe.

I posted this dreaming of the day I would scoop up my daughter Hope. I believed. Her nest was ready and so was our family of three, eager to grow to four. Because I'd experienced meeting Haley Joy for the first time, blueprints existed for the explosion of love I'd soon feel seeing Hope. Still, my heart was bursting with excitement, knowing every love, every soul, is unique, and I would soon lock eyes with my amazing baby girl.

March 13

Instead of that anxiety about chasing a passion that you're not even feeling, do something that's a lot simpler: just follow your curiosity.
— Elizabeth Gilbert

I've always thought it's better to be interested in other people rather than trying so hard to be interesting. Taking the focus off amassing our own awesomeness clears the way to look around, to see what and who might spark a new idea or outlook. Be curious today. Something might be hiding in plain sight!

Rest and self-care are so important. When you take time to replenish your spirit, it allows you to serve others from the overflow. You cannot serve from an empty vessel.

— Eleanor Brown

Finding time is the hard part, right? Let's try, though. Check your vessel!

MARCH 15

Date someone who is a home and an adventure all at once.

This is Joel to me. He is not only my permanent address, he's the guy who always says yes when I ask, "Honey, do you want to [fill in anything here]?" I'll say, "If we go to Rehoboth Beach, you'll be sleeping on a blow-up mattress." YES. "Can we steal away for a few days when your schedule is this nuts?" YES. "I know you're exhausted, but do you want to go for a walk with me?" YES. My man is game and I love that.

March 16

He has made everything beautiful in its time.

— *Ecclesiastes* 3:11

My co-host on *Today,* Savannah Guthrie, says this quote provides two things when she reads it: perspective and relief. Just eight words are an instant reminder that a force greater than her is sovereign over events and even time itself. "I have my plans, my hopes, my intentions, but God holds me. His plans for me are generous and trustworthy, even when I think He might be running a bit late," she says. "Always, His blessings are right on time."

March 17

St. Patrick's Day is an enchanted time —
a day to begin transforming winter's
dreams into summer's magic.

— Adrienne Cook

The St. Patrick's Day Parade in New York
City is always a blast. I love that everyone is
so happy, feeling lucky in their leprechaun
suits. If you're in Manhattan on St. Patty's
Day, chances are you're going to get hugged
by someone dressed in green. (Or pinched
if you're not!)

March 18

90% of parenting is peeling clementines
and lying about what time it is.
— Bunmi Laditan (@BunmiLaditan)

Clementine peels . . . on my counter . . .
right now! Oh, and it's "nap time," honey.

MARCH 19

Spring is nature's way of saying, "Let's party!"

— Robin Williams

Yes! I love that feeling of sunrays kissing my exposed skin for the first time in months. Let's get this party started, spring!

MARCH 20

My ability to remember song lyrics from the '80s far exceeds my ability to remember why I walked into the kitchen.

Here's what I'm picturing: freshman and sophomore year in the Slusher wing of my dorm at Virginia Tech blasting Lionel Richie's "Hello" on a cassette player, and my poor roommate Kelly thinking, *Oh Lord, please, not again . . .*

MARCH 21

I wonder how much of what weighs me
down is not mine to carry.

— ADITI

I'm a control freak on the little things. I like
to be sure of what I'm doing and when so I
can do my best. But when I got sick, instantly I let go of trying to manage the big
things. I surrendered. *God, you got this. Hala
has it too.* I remember doctors wanted me
to look at the different types of surgery I
could have and I said, "Nope. I'm not doing it." When Hala asked me, I said the
same thing. There were so many big deci-
sions to make and I just let the pros in my
life figure it out. *I'm not in charge.* The feeling of freedom that relinquishing control
gave me was a relief. I think it's a good idea
to check what we're carrying around that's
out of our control. Check today?

MARCH 22

Imperfection is fine.
— Anna Wintour

I've got imperfection down. Found a plastic fork inside my wallet the other day . . . ??

only thing Brett plays chase with is that adorable pup, Edgar.

MARCH 23

Change your thoughts and you can change your world.
— Norman Vincent Peale

Brett Eldredge is totally into two things: his dog, Edgar, and meditation. Both have changed him for the better, companions that help him live a better life. The country singer-songwriter says he's long struggled with anxiety, but that once he learned to meditate, negative thoughts lost all of their power. "I figured out how much we chase the millions of thoughts we have every day, and you can either chase down those negative thoughts or you can see them as they are and look at them in a different way." Brett says by rejecting the worries and worst-case scenarios in his brain, he's learned to love and accept himself. "I'm enjoying life a lot more," he says. Now the only thing Brett plays chase with is that adorable pup, Edgar.

MARCH 24

It's time for trust and surrender.

During one of my first visits to four-year-old Leah Still in the hospital, I couldn't believe how calm her parents were. Their daughter had been diagnosed with neuroblastoma stage IV cancer, but they were smiling when I walked into the room. *How in the world are they doing this?* I knew Devon and Channing were people of strong faith, but clearly so many of us would be a puddle beside the bed. Not those two — backs straight, welcoming words, bald daughter sitting happily before them. Fast-forward to now, and the trust and surrender I saw in that room have had beautiful results. Leah remains in remission and has a message for other kids battling cancer: "I would say stay strong and it doesn't matter what's on the outside, it matters what's on

the inside," she says. "And you're not fighting this alone, ever."

114

MARCH 25

If she doesn't text you when she's drunk, you ain't the one.

Well . . . maybe she meant to but fell asleep.

Look in the mirror. That's your competition.

— Eric Thomas

To me, this is my *Today* colleague Meredith Vieira. She plays her own game and always has. I admire her because she's never looked at other people and thought, *I need to be like that.* She does her own thing. Nearly every job she's taken, Meredith has left on her own terms. In our business, where spots are so coveted and people hold on to their chairs with white knuckles, my dear friend Meredith comes and goes with grace. I love that.

MARCH 27

Growth is painful. Change is painful. But nothing is as painful as staying stuck somewhere you don't belong.
— Mandy Hale

Sometimes we just say, "I'm *over* it!" We have to get so sick of where we are that pain seems like a good trade for a way out of the wrong space.

MARCH 28

Before you speak, let your words pass through three gates: At the first gate, ask yourself, "Is it true?" At the second gate ask, "Is it necessary?" At the third gate ask, "Is it kind?"

— Adapted from "Three Gates"
by Beth Day

Wouldn't the world be a better place if we each paused and asked ourselves these questions before we said something? It seems like a lot to think through, though. But maybe if we do it often enough, it simply becomes second nature.

MARCH 29

Fall on your back.
— Patricia Russell-McCloud

At a breakfast conference I went to one year while I was working in New Orleans, a dynamic speaker named Patricia Russell-McCloud gave a rousing talk about being resilient in life. A powerhouse at the podium, she said, "If you fall — and trust me, you will — make sure you fall on your back. Because if you fall on your back, you can see up. And if you can *see* up, you can *get* up. And you can keep going and going and going." I just like that image; much more positive than a face-plant.

March 30

So what. Now what?
— Linda Cliatt-Wayman

One of the most powerful TED talks I've ever watched was delivered by Linda Cliatt-Wayman. In it, she lays out her approach, as a new principal, to turning around a dangerous, low-performing public school in North Philadelphia, the area where she was once a student. The entire talk is amazing, but I love *this* particular quote. Linda explains that when presented with every-thing that was wrong with the school and its students, she boldly said, "So what. Now what?" Basically, what are we going to do to make it right? And there's so much more to love about her. As principal, here's how she always ended daily announcements to the kids: "If nobody told you they loved you today, remember I do and I always will." Incredible, right? No surprise, the school and its students made remarkable strides under her leadership. Linda has inspired so many, including one online viewer who wrote this in the comment section below the TED talk: *I literally stood up and clapped while alone in my living room after watching this.*

MARCH 31

When your past calls, don't answer. It has nothing new to say.

You already know what it's going to tell you: blah, blah, blah. Let it go to voicemail. Instead, your future's calling. Pick up!

APRIL 1

Be grateful for the tiny details of your life and make room for unexpected and beautiful blessings.

— Henry Van Dyke

When Joel and I moved into our apartment together and we were waiting for our first baby — for God to send us Haley — I imagined that the spare bedroom upstairs would be the nursery. Because we had no idea when or if an adoption would happen, Joel suggested we use the room for his office in the meantime. I said, "Oh no, we can't. We have to make space for the baby." I feel like sometimes we fill all of our spaces. Maybe look around today . . . see what might be blocking the next best thing that could happen for you.

P.S. A month later we got the call that Haley had arrived!

April 2

Don't give up what you want most, for what you want now.

Instant gratification, you are so devious. Please leave us alone! Call me crazy, but one trick I have with food is laundry detergent. I can't trust myself not to Dumpster-dive when it comes to anything sweet — like what's left of an Entenmann's cake — so I'll douse it with Tide or Cascade to stop the madness.

APRIL 3

Today I want you to think about all that
you are instead of all that you are *not.*

This reminds me of Gillian Lynne, a woman
whose nickname as a child was Wriggle Bottom. She grew up in England during the
1930s and wore out her parents and teachers with her constant motion and inability
to focus. ("ADHD" wasn't a term yet.)
Finally, a doctor dealing with Gillian left his
office to speak with her mother but turned
on a radio before he slipped out. Miraculously, from the hallway, both adults
watched as Gillian danced and twirled
about in the room, moved by the music. The
doctor looked at Gillian's mother and said,
"Your daughter's not sick, she's a dancer."
Wriggle Bottom went on to have a successful career as a principal in the Royal Ballet,
a director, and a choreographer behind such

legendary theater productions as *Cats* and *The Phantom of the Opera*.

April 4

When you're right, be quiet.
— Deeksha Joshi

Exactly. And don't even do a little dance in the other room. Not cool.

APRIL 5

Sometimes when we are called to obey, the fear does not subside and we are expected to move against the fear. One must choose to do it afraid.

— Elisabeth Elliot

That had to be the case in 2004 when news legend Connie Chung delivered a speech at a conference for the Asian American Journalists Association in Washington, DC. After I introduced her, Connie stepped up to the podium and said, "I have a little song for you guys." That year, then Senator John Kerry and President George W. Bush had both addressed the attendees. So, Connie began singing, "Bush and Kerry, Bush and Kerry" — really belting it out — to the tune of "Love and Marriage." Everyone in the audience was quiet, staring at her. What in the world? Because I was standing behind her, I had the point of view of being Connie. I was pitting out for her! Still, she kept at it. She sang even louder and finished strong. And to my surprise and delight, Connie had won over the room. The crowd burst into applause! That day taught me how important it is to stick with something you commit to, even if you feel half nuts.

APRIL 6

See rejection as redirection.

Chalk up twenty-seven rejections for me before I got hired as a broadcast journalist. And y'know what? I ended up right where I needed to begin.

External clutter is internal clutter on display.

Gulp. If this is true, I'm a hot mess! In spring 2019, Clea Shearer and Joanna Teplin — the moms behind a Nashville-based organizing business called the Home Edit — tackled the chaotic clothes closet in my apartment. I can't believe they stayed once they opened it. From unused ski pants to countless New Orleans Saints T-shirts to tennis balls and coffee mugs, my bed was overloaded with no's. No, we're not keeping those. Pepcid, Craisins, cruise brochures, and single shoes didn't deter this dynamic duo. Somehow, with an array of organizational tips and tricks, they whipped my closet into shape. Every nook and cranny was home to something. I could see all of my journals at once for the first time in my life! I was overjoyed, but secretly I felt terrible. *I'm going to ruin all of this shortly.* I gotta say, their hard work and genius system prevailed a lot longer than I thought it would. But . . . I'm glad I took a photo of what it once looked like. #Goals.

April 8

We were together. I forget the rest.
— Walt Whitman

I have a sweet memory that unfolded when I was standing with a guy next to the fountain at Lincoln Center. He was holding his phone in one hand, and with the other he gave me the left speaker of his earbuds. With both of us listening to the Jack Johnson song "Better Together," we started dancing, the water bubbling beside us. There was something so special about that tiny little moment.

APRIL 9

If you want to change the world, go home and love your family.
— Saint Teresa of Calcutta

This just cuts through all the noise, doesn't it? How about today, when you're with someone you love, ask them to dance. Before you get to the business of dinner or bills or homework, take a little three-minute spin around the living room; create a little magic.

APRIL 10

Sometimes music is the only medicine the heart and soul need.

After my dad died, my brother and I sat in front of the record player for hours, playing James Taylor songs over and over and over again. There's just something so soothing about his voice and lyrics. Adel and I were both numb with grief, resetting the needle on the record was about the only movement we could muster.

APRIL 11

My father said there were two kinds of
people in the world: givers and takers.
The takers may eat better, but the givers
sleep better.
— MARLO THOMAS

You can't hear "St. Jude Children's Research Hospital" without thinking of Danny
Thomas, its founder, or his daughter,
Marlo. Every time I see Marlo she starts
our conversation with, "Here's the latest
breakthrough . . ." Not, "Hi, how are you
doing?" She's laser focused on saving kids
battling cancer. When Marlo invited me to
visit the hospital in Memphis, I thought,
*Brace yourself. This is going to be the most
heartbreaking, terribly sad thing in the world.*
Thankfully, it was far from it. Upon arriving, I met a little girl who took my hand
and said, "C'mon, let's look around." The
paint colors were bright, the vibe was

energetic, and the kids were full of hope. After the visit, I could only imagine how great it was to work there! *That's* how inspiring St. Jude is. Marlo and everyone involved with the hospital are truly some of the greatest givers in this world.

APRIL 12

Sometimes renewal comes in surrender.
— Rob Bell

This is such a lovely breath of fresh spring air. May today be a new beginning in some way for you.

APRIL 13

Remember why you started.
— Ralph Marston

One day, the gun went off and you started running as fast as you could. There was something important on the other side of that finish line . . . do you remember? Yes! Now keep going, champion!

Relax. Everything is running right on schedule.

— The Universe

When I met Joel, I was nearly forty-nine years old, divorced, and buried in work hosting the fourth hour of *Today* with Kathie Lee. It happened because my friend and *Today* producer Joanne La Marca asked me to speak at an evening event. Honestly, I didn't want to go. The trip was a long, rainy drive to the tip of Manhattan and I was tired. Still, I agreed and brought copies of my latest book. The room was tiny and filled with about thirty men in suits, Wall Street guys. *Drat.* My crowd is the Junior League! After enduring what I'm sure was a snooze-fest speech, a few guys asked me to sign books. "Can you make it to my meemaw?" (See? A Junior Leaguer would have asked me to sign it to *her.*) When the next guy asked for a signature, I thought, *Here we go . . . to Nana.* "Sure. Who should I sign it to?" He said, "How about to me?" On the drive home, I joked with Joanne through texts about the low energy at the event. I also texted, "Who's Joel?" She responded, "I'm on it." And she was. An email exchange was followed by a dinner date and now six years together and counting. I'm so glad we met, Joel, right on schedule.

APRIL 15

Running away from any problem only
increases the distance from the solution.

Like when I put off doing my taxes, and
then one day in October I find myself running after the nearest UPS truck like a
maniac. "Please stooooop!" I scream, pant-
ing and waving my packet of procrastina-
tion in the air.

April 16

The people who are meant to be in your life are the ones who know how to gently wait for you to heal.

I can still picture my mom's friend Linda Stubbs lying in bed with her right after my dad died. When Adel and I rushed home, that's what we saw. I'm pretty sure Linda was the one who broke the news to Adel, too, because my mom couldn't. She and Linda have been friends now for forty years.

APRIL 17

Hello, Miss Haley! We've waited so long for you.

— My mom

This is what my mom said to Haley the first time they met. A sign hangs in Haley's room featuring these sweet words. I can't believe I get to share Haley with her teta, the beautiful woman who raised me.

The greatest weapon against stress is our
ability to choose one thought over another.
— William James

I love the story of Maya Angelou living in
San Francisco when she was a teenager. At
sixteen, she wanted desperately to become a
street-car attendant. From the formfitting
uniforms to the change-making machines,
she loved everything she saw about the
women who worked aboard the streetcars.
The challenge was — all of the women were
white. No one would even provide Maya
with an application. When she shared her
disappointment with her mother, her mom
told her to *go get the job.* "Sit there every
day and read one of your big, thick Russian
books," she said. "Get there before the
secretaries arrive and don't leave until they
do." Maya recalled how the staff laughed at
her and made unkind remarks, but still, she

showed up every day for two weeks. Then one morning, a man came out of his office and asked her why she wanted the job. When she told him of her love for the uniforms and for people, he gave her the job! Maya said the experience taught her everything she needed to know about dedication and determination.

APRIL 19

If you never try, you'll never know what you're capable of.

— John Barrow

The gifted actress Taraji P. Henson has got this one down. She is *amazing.* Taraji is such a bright light, and when you interview her she makes you feel like she doesn't want to leave. I've watched her share the story of moving to Los Angeles to pursue acting with seven hundred dollars and a toddler. People in her life told her she was crazy, reckless, and too old at twenty-six. But she ran toward her dream anyway. "If I didn't," she says, "what was I teaching my son?" She says she refused to allow the fears of other people to hold her back. That same determination had fueled her when she got pregnant in college and people warned her that she'd never graduate. "I walked across that stage with my son on my hip and I collected my diploma," she says. Now in her late forties, Taraji says she's just getting started and is excited to explore what's next. Thank you, Taraji, for showing us why it's *so* important to try.

APRIL 20

Staying vulnerable is a risk we have to take if we want to experience connection.
— Brené Brown

TRUST is the backbone here, right? *I trust you with my exposed heart and mind.* But what if the other person doesn't offer the same? Maybe we're supposed to show them how.

APRIL 21

People will never remember what you said or what you did, but they'll never forget how you made them feel.
— CARL W. BUEHNER

Every day. That's how often Michael Bublé says he lives his life with this quote in mind. (Maya Angelou is often associated with this quote, which I love.) While he admits some people may be cynical about his outlook, he solidly believes it's important to realize how much power each and every person has in this life. "You get to decide every morning when you wake up," he says, "to change lives . . . with a smile, a compliment, a hug. I just love that you have that kind of power and you can use it for good."

APRIL 22

The best apology is changed behavior.

Ain't that the truth. "Walk the walk" comes to mind . . .

(Pro tip: don't ever say "I'm sorry you feel that way.")

APRIL 23

Remove all sugars from your diet to avoid unnecessary calories and any joy you may be feeling.

This sums up my fear when Jennifer Lopez challenged me to a ten-day no-sugar, low-carb diet. Of course I accepted (it's J. Lo!) and my plan was to make the menu easy: chicken, vegetables, eggs, repeat. I then removed all sugary things from my house because I simply can't be trusted. Surprisingly, besides boring the heck out of my taste buds, the initial stretch wasn't too hard, barring two slipups: alcohol and Coffee Mate. Then day six nearly broke me. In my mind, I was devouring endless sugar-carb combos (think glazed doughnuts and chocolate-covered potato chips). My *Today* pal Carson Daly even tried to bribe me, saying he'd make a donation to my favorite charity if I took a bite of a massive crumb cake. Still, I finished strong and rewarded myself with a Super Bowl Sunday snack binge. Of course, Jennifer crushed her challenge and vowed to repeat it right away. Go, J. Lo! (But please don't call me again about this because I can't say no to you.)

APRIL 24

Wisdom is the reward you get for a lifetime
of listening when you'd have preferred to
talk.

— Doug Larson

When Frank Gifford died, I decided *not* to
listen to Kathie Lee. I was flying home from
celebrating my birthday in 2015 when I got
word that Frank had passed. During my
phone call with Kathie Lee, she told me not
to drive out to Connecticut to see her; she
was okay. But I decided to head out to her
house when I landed. I'll never forget walking out to her back porch and seeing Kath
facing the water, her back to me. When she
turned and saw me, she said, "I'm so glad
you don't listen to me, Hoda."

APRIL 25

You can't start the next chapter of your
life if you keep rereading the last one.

To me this one is like the girl who's still
secretly talking to her old boyfriend all the
time, wondering why she can't meet anyone.
C'mon. Clear the decks.

April 26

You can, you should, and if you're brave enough to start, you will.

— Stephen King

I think Stephen King just threw down. Are you up for the challenge today?

Give every day the chance to become the most beautiful day of your life.
— Mark Twain

Is today that day? If not, then it may just be tomorrow.

April 28

You're always one decision away from a totally different life.

—Mark Twain

I love country star Thomas Rhett and his beautiful wife, Lauren. When you're with them, they feel like family or neighbors, whipping out their phones to show you photos of their darling kids. This quote reminds me of the story he tells of how close they were to marrying other people. The two met in grade school, dated in high school, and broke things off in college, remaining dear friends throughout. In their twenties, both dated people they thought they'd marry. But Thomas says that one day, Lauren's father called him. "He said, 'If you don't come over here tonight and tell Lauren how you feel about her, then I'm going to tell her how you feel about her.' " The two were engaged just months later! Without

that one decision — and a bit of a nudge —
their lives would have been totally different.

Love the people God gave you, because
He will need them back one day.
                                    — Becky Kinder

My friend Janie says she chose this quote
because of how simply it delivers such a
powerful message. "The first time I read
this, my heart just dropped. The reality of
that *one day* makes you want to sit in a
corner and gargle on your tears," she says.
"But the quote also serves as a kick in the
pants. It's a reminder to make sure the
people we love know how lucky we feel to
have them beside us each day." Janie's a
lover. She loves hard. The only problem
with people who love so hard is that they
feel loss more deeply than most of us. When
she was thirty-four, Jane lost her mom to a
traumatic brain injury. Years later, she
watched Parkinson's disease steal her father
away. God wanted both parents back, I

guess. The best part about Janie is that despite the unbearable pain, she keeps on loving, and I thank God for that.

April 30

Your fear of looking stupid is holding you back.

In 2015, I competed on *Lip Sync Battle* against beloved television host and former New York Giants player Michael Strahan. The show had recently debuted, so I didn't know much about it. I'd chosen two songs, I knew the lyrics . . . that's about it. When I entered the studio, I noticed bleachers. *Um, is there an audience?* Then someone said, "You're going to have dancers, and meet your choreographer." *Whaaaaaaat?* I was terrified. When Michael walked in to run through his song, "Poison," he was flanked by Bell Biv DeVoe, the group that sings it! Really? Before I knew it I was mouthing, "Oh my God, Becky, look at her butt," the intro to "Baby Got Back." Then Michael slayed, and I was dressed in gold chains, aviators, and a pink suit for "Uptown

Funk." For that song, something hit me. I decided to just have fun . . . to pretend I was in my living room going nuts to Bruno Mars. That changed everything! To put it in terms of Michael's world, I left it all on the field.

MAY 1

Some days, I barely have the strength to get out of bed and face the world with the pain of losing you hidden behind a smile.

There are so many among us who struggle mightily each day simply to show up. Just getting out of bed is a challenge. The idea of doing more than getting through the day is almost impossible. For those of you nursing hidden hurts today, know you are not alone. If this is you, we honor your strength. If this isn't you, be kind and remember those who may be having a tough time. We're all in this together!

MAY 2

I don't mind getting wrinkles if it's from laughing and spending time in the sunshine.

And let's throw in sleep lines from an awesome nap! By the way, that whole thing about "You sleep when the baby sleeps" is a myth . . . because you can't. While the baby sleeps, you wash the bottles, throw clothes in the dryer, and clean up the disasters. Then, the minute you're done — actually, the second you're done — you hear *Waaaaaaaaa!* blasting from the baby monitor. That's when *you* start to cry. You cry when the baby cries. When Joel or the babysitter is home, I will head upstairs for a nap. I take a sleeve of Oreos with me, pull down the blackout shades, and it's over. Two or three hours later, I'm back . . . a different person after some *z*'s.

May 3

Sunsets are proof, endings can be
beautiful too!
— Beau Taplin

I posted this on the morning of Kathie Lee's last day with me on the fourth hour of *Today.* She is an absolute master at embracing what's next! I think it's because she has so many ideas. The yellow pad in her car is filled with notes about "the next thing" — plans for a Broadway show, a movie, a book, a product line. Before Kath left our show for good, she'd already bought a home in Nashville and was creating music there with songwriters. Her "next" was already under way! For Kathie Lee, endings are simply the beginning of something new.

May 4

You've always had the power . . . [you] had to learn it for [your]self.
— Glinda, *The Wizard of Oz*

Sometimes we have to relearn it, too. We've got the power!

May 5

No one can make you feel inferior without
your consent.

— Eleanor Roosevelt

There are so many meaningful quotes attributed to former First Lady Eleanor Roosevelt, and this one perhaps reflects what
she eventually learned herself. After Eleanor lost both parents by age ten, the mater-
nal grandmother who raised her apparently
did so with a harsh tongue. After marrying
Franklin Delano Roosevelt, Eleanor faced
criticism again, belittled by her controlling
mother-in-law. Marital strife caused more
hurt, but throughout Eleanor's life, she
bolstered her self-esteem through writing,
fighting for social change, traveling the
world, and sharing powerful words . . . like
these.

今today’s Ms. Oliver’s question reads like a beautiful challenge.

May 6

Tell me, what is it you plan to do with your one wild and precious life?

— Mary Oliver

Those words — "wild and precious." There's something about them that makes you see life as a gift, not a grind. Since my battle with cancer, I've tried to live in a way that would . . . let's say . . . please Mary Oliver. Early on in my cancer journey, four words became my secret weapon to a more purposeful life: "You can't scare me." I wrote that sentence in my journal almost every day. The new me was fearless and I felt wildly free. I decided to meet separately with the CEO of NBC and the news division president, asking both to consider me for the new fourth hour of *Today*. I landed the position and it changed my professional life forever. To me (and perhaps to you

169

today), Ms. Oliver's question reads like a beautiful challenge.

MAY 7

Once you've seen a woman take her bra off without removing her shirt, it makes more sense why they should be in charge of things.

Not to mention seeing her catch a dropped phone in midair after tripping over a teddy bear in her six-inch heels while holding a screaming toddler. Women have skills.

May 8

Don't be surprised how quickly the universe moves once you've decided.

A decision is motion, like the first domino falling. This reminds me of how quickly things moved for Joel and me once I said — out loud — that I wanted to try adopting a baby with him. That was November 2017, and news of Haley arrived two months later.

United States. It took me a while, but eventually I saw okay with being different. In fact, I was proud to be different.

MAY 9

You'll turn out ordinary if you're not careful.

— Ann Brashares

I felt far from ordinary during my grammar school years; I felt painfully different. My name was hard to pronounce and my parents' accent was hard to understand. My wild hair and darker skin set me apart, too. Throw in some octagon-shaped glasses and you've got a *looooong* school year. It took me until high school — or maybe even college — to realize that my Egyptian heritage was actually pretty cool. I was moving through life on the backs of incredibly strong and accomplished relatives. My great-aunt was the first female attorney in Egypt, my grandmother among the first female physicians. Because of the strength and smarts of my parents, my siblings and I were living a life full of potential in the

United States. It took me a while, but
eventually I was okay with being different . . . in fact, I was proud to be, too.

May 10

We came from Mama's heart.
— HALEY AND HOPE

It's a question that comes up when you grow your family through adoption. "Where did I come from?" I always say to Haley, "You didn't come from Mommy's tummy, you came from my . . ." She fills in the blank with "heart." That's why these words were written on my Mother's Day card the first year I was blessed to have both Haley and Hope in my life.

MAY 11

Remember the days you prayed for the things you have now.

Talk about a good reminder to be grateful. The things we once went to our knees for can so easily be overlooked or considered ho-hum.

MAY 12

A ship in port is safe, but that's not what ships are built for.

—John A. Shedd

My sense of job security and happiness peaked when I worked in New Orleans. I fell in love with the city instantly . . . from the minute my future news director bought us drive-through margaritas during the interview process. The six years I spent at WWL-TV were spectacular, and I knew the only reason I'd leave was for a role at the network. In late 1997, that opportunity arrived. I interviewed for a position at *Dateline* NBC and was offered the job. The decision before me was two-pronged: Do I leave my happy place for a lesser-paying job I could get fired from in six months? Or do I ignore a dream come true and regret it for the rest of my life? In the end, the image of me on a barstool blabbing about my "shot at the bigs that got away" was unacceptable. I chose instead to leave the port . . . to head out into the open sea. Turns out, I made the right call. I love my life in New York City and I visit New Orleans whenever I can. (My heart still pounds when I fly in.) Yes, taking a risk can be scary, but to me — living with what-if is worse.

Thankfully, they finally did, Amy — you're not only fearless, you're the best.

MAY 13

Listening is often the only thing needed to help someone.

I'm certainly grateful that the bosses at NBC listened to Amy Rosenblum. The brand-new fourth hour of *Today* was evolving and Amy, as its executive producer, was working behind the scenes to land me a seat on that set. Amy had always been my ally, encouraging me to improve on air, be more myself. She actually told me once — during a commercial break on another hour — that the bosses thought I was boring. Huh? I was stunned. "Just be the girl in my office," she'd coax. So, when it came time to name hosts for the fourth hour, Amy told the executives she felt I was right for the job. They weren't sold, but she didn't back down. "Fire me if she doesn't work out." It gets better. Pistol Amy then said, "Strap on your vaginas, boys, and *listen* to me."

Thankfully, they finally did. Amy — you're not only fearless, you're the best!

MAY 14

Happiness is the best makeup to emphasize your inner beauty and outer glow.
— Debasish Mridha

What he said (and keratin). If you have unruly hair, you're nodding right now. If you don't, we're happy for you, but please count not only your blessings, but all the money you *don't* spend on Hair Management. My mop has always been something that needs to be . . . addressed. I used to shell out countless dollars on products that promised to smooth, condition, mend, trick, and temporarily wrangle my frizzy mane. Regularly scheduled blowouts served as my Xanax — when my hair was right, all was right in the world. Then (angels sing) keratin hit the market. Mysterious, miraculous keratin. I still can't believe how it's changed my life! After every treatment, my hair is as soft as it is straight. I can actually swing it, Farrah-style (sort of), a childhood dream fulfilled. Some people worry about what's in keratin, I worry about a shortage. Can we run low on keratin like we did helium that one year? Please say no. Actually, I'm not worried. I'd still find a way. (Call me, Pancho.)

May 15

There are moments which mark your life. Moments when you realize nothing will ever be the same and time is divided into two parts — before this and after this.
— John Hobbes, *Fallen*

This feeling was so vivid for me during my predawn flight to pick up Haley for the first time. "I Choose You" by Sara Bareilles was playing in my headphones and despite my seat belt, I was floating. As I watched the sun rise, I knew it was not only the start of a new day, it was the *first* day of a new life for me — for us. Soon, I would hold my daughter and lock eyes with her. Motherhood was waiting for me. Time was dividing. Every minute we flew took me further away from before and brought me ever closer to after.

May 16

Never in the history of calming down has anyone calmed down by being told to calm down.

Gasoline, match, and . . . . BOOM.

MAY 17

Everything can change in an instant. Everything. And then there is only before and after.
— PHYLLIS REYNOLDS NAYLOR

In the blink of an eye, things can change. We've all had Mondays that brought us news — good or bad — that never crossed our mind on Sunday night.

MAY 18

The best way to predict your future is to **create it.**

Let's stop gazing into that crystal ball and look in the mirror. *That's* who's in charge of the future!

MAY 19

Always remember to fall asleep with a dream and wake up with a purpose.

I'm just relieved when I wake up on time! To make sure I do, I have three alarms set on my phone: 3:00, 3:05, 3:15 a.m. You may use the same system — backups to the backups! The sound of the alarm that wakes me is important, too. I use one called "Silk," soothing but effective.

May 20

Action is the antidote to despair.
— Joan Baez

On the hardest days, it's easy to feel mired in the tar, stuck. Still, I believe in this quote. With all your might, do *something* . . . even if it's reaching your hand up, asking for help.

May 21

You wouldn't worry so much about what other people think if you realized how seldom they do.

— Olin Miller

Truth! In the pursuit of happiness and sanity, let's try hard to be warriors, not worriers.

People who show you new music are
important.

Carson Daly is one of those people. The
other day he pulled me aside and said,
"Hoda, you've got to listen to this . . . it's
Kelly Clarkson singing 'Princess of China'
on the BBC!" He always has something
unique to share. Carson's a music guy, so
he finds songs you won't hear on Top 40
radio. I've always loved being exposed to
new music. When someone comes to you
with a song, they're thinking about you . . .
they want to share a feeling with you. Now,
do I sometimes overshare? Maybe. I feel
sorry for Laura and Mary in the makeup
room because I always walk in saying, "Oh
my God, you guys . . . listen, listen, listen!"
I feel like *I've* written the song, that I own
it. And I'm slightly offended if someone
reacts with, "Meh. It's not for me." What

are you talking about? Of course it's for you!
Let's listen to it again . . .

May 23

Oh dear! I really ought to do something.
But I am already in my pajamas.
— Professor Hubert J. Farnsworth,
Futurama

. . . said me, at eight p.m.

May 24

The funny thing about kids is, they are the reason we lose it and the reason we hold it together.

True! We pull out our hair *and* we put on our big-girl pants. All because of kiddos. I remember a phase Haley went through when she was taking off all of her clothes — including her diaper — and putting them away. I'd walk by the video monitor and see her lying on the floor of her room, naked. "What's going on, honey?" I'd ask. "Mommy, my clothes in the hamper, diaper in the pail." And then began the struggle to get her dressed again. The battle was ugly. I'd resort to letting her play with an app on my phone called Bubbles, so that touching the screen — popping bubbles — would distract her as she screamed, "No diaper, Mama!" As I persisted, I'd say, "I'm *begging* you, Haley." I said it so many times that she began to say it back to me, giggling through the tug-of-war. "Begging you, Mommy, begging you." Ha! I couldn't help but laugh along with her. (Most of the time.)

MAY 25

This nation will remain the land of the free only so long as it is the home of the brave.
— Elmer Davis

God bless the men and women — and their families — who sacrifice for us, near and far. We love you.

May 26

It is better to know how to learn than to know.

— Dr. Seuss

The doc is thinking long-term, right? Knowing is a dead end. Learning knows no end. Joel's sweet sister, Beth, sent Haley all of the Dr. Seuss books she read as a child . . . the very same ones. I love that they're worn by the hands of Beth's young self, flipping through the pages and poring over the pictures and rhymes. Right now, Elmo is Haley's go-to guy, but someday soon I know she'll dive into Dr. Seuss books and add them to her "Mommy, again" list.

MAY 27

The beginning is the most important part
of the work.

— Plato

Words of wisdom from BC! Begin — other-
wise there is no middle or end.

May 28

"Did you eat yet?" has to be one of the most romantic questions ever.

Whenever Joel makes me my favorite meal — before I take the first bite — he says, "I'm going to cook this for you for the rest of your life." Mmm, honey.

P.S. The meal is grilled salmon with special secret spices, sautéed spinach with garlic, and a perfectly baked potato.

MAY 29

If we want to raise helpers, we have to be helpers.

— Chris Jordan

Stephanie Ruhle, my colleague at NBC, covered the story of young adults engaged in what's known as "impact" travel. In 2018, college students from around the country spent their spring breaks in the US Virgin Islands helping to rebuild homes and remove debris following two hurricanes that devastated the area. Even Steph joined in, bringing her three children with her to donate books to a damaged elementary school. I like the concept of carving out time during a trip or vacation to help out the local community. Seems like a great idea for a family tradition. Our kids are watching us . . . . everywhere.

May 30

Be the person you want to meet.

I lived in New Orleans when I went through a breakup. The whole experience was rough, and I felt like crap. You may know the feeling. One day, while I was waiting on the dryer in my local laundromat, a police officer walked in. I must have looked like crap too, because he asked if I was okay. I said, "No . . . I'm not." For some reason, I was honest with him. We started talking, and eventually began dating. Looking back, Matt was exactly who and what I needed; he was a rescuer. But as time passed and I became stronger, we weren't the right fit anymore. He was still a rescuer, but I didn't need to be saved. Now each of us is with the person we were meant to meet. I'm so happy for Matt. He was and still is such a great guy.

May 31

Learn to say **"NO"** without explaining yourself.

I'm such a work in progress on this one!
  Me: "No. But I mean, I can try to . . .
except I'm slammed, so . . . I really can't
because . . . [pause] . . . let me double-
check."

JUNE 1

After all the eating I've done this winter, I'm happy to report my flip-flops still fit.

Slipped right into 'em!

JUNE 2

You are the author of your story. If you're stuck on the same page, remember that at any moment, you have the power to write a new chapter.

Remi Adeleke *is* this quote. I met him for the first time at Neary's, a pub on New York City's East Side. I felt like I was getting to know the best of Remi, because that's all he brings to the table. With him, there's no pretense . . . just humility and kindness. Remi's remarkable story spans from a wildly privileged childhood in Nigeria, to a drug arrest in the Bronx, to becoming a celebrated Navy SEAL. (He first had to learn how to swim!) It takes his book, *Transformed: A Navy SEAL's Unlikely Journey from the Throne of Africa, to the Streets of the Bronx, to Defying All Odds,* to cover the breadth of his personal evolution, fueled by his mother's mantra — and her example —

that hard work makes anything possible. Now married with three sons and a home in Southern California, Remi has added "actor" to his life's work. I love that he landed a role in the movie *Transformers,* because he is one.

JUNE 3

When you're tempted to lose patience with someone, think about how patient God has been with you all the time.

When I was single, I remember an expert suggesting that I jot down a few qualities I was looking for in a man. One I listed was: "I need a man with infinite patience." Well, thank goodness I found Joel. How many times has he heard me say, "Where's my phone? Have you seen my phone, honey?" Every time, he looks around for it . . . in the same three places where I always lose track of it. Or he'll just stand back as I suddenly swirl around the apartment like a tornado, trying to solve something. "Anyway, where were we?" he'll say, getting us back on track. Joel is very neat, and I'm very not. Even when I try to contain my mess, something is missing because of me. "Hey . . ." he'll say kindly, "I'm looking for my blue jacket . . ." Of course he is, because it's buried under dry cleaning, a baby-shower gift, and a diaper bag that I've hung on the coatrack! I know how lucky I am, Joel. Thank you for your endless patience with me.

JUNE 4

Someone else's opinion of you is NONE of your business.

— Rachel Hollis

A lot of us can relate to singer Trisha Yearwood's struggle with criticism on social media: "I'll read a hundred nice things about me and if I read one thing that's negative, I'm just focused on that." But a breakthrough came for her while reading the book *Girl, Wash Your Face* by Rachel Hollis. When she read the quote "Someone else's opinion of you is none of your business," the words were affirming. "You've got to live your life," Trisha explained. "You've got to do what you do. You can't let what someone else thinks of you define you." She's now changed the way she interacts on social media: "I read until I get to something negative and then leave. I just let it go." With daughters in their twenties, Trisha tries to offer them perspective on negativity. "It's tough, especially at that age. We have that conversation a lot. It's hard to tell a young girl that everything she reads is not the worst thing in the world and that it doesn't really matter. I hope they learn that you can't be defined by it."

JUNE 5

Not all storms come to disrupt your life, some come to clear your path.

True, but it's not so easy to figure this one out as we're being pelted in the face with cold, hard reality. Hindsight, we wish you'd show up earlier.

JUNE 6

It's rigged–everything, in your favor.
— RUMI

This reminds me of the line in the poem "Desiderata" that reads, ". . . the universe is unfolding as it should." I think the idea is to try to live your life believing that everything — both good and bad — is happening because *something* behind the scenes has your back.

JUNE 7

Trust me, you can dance.
— Vodka

Liar. — Next Morning

JUNE 8

One day you will need the same grace that you will not give someone else.

Probably, but in the middle of feeling angry we think, *I'd never do to anyone what you did to me!* Why pay it forward when we're never going to misbehave in the same way? But the truth is, we'll all probably need a little forgiveness, a little empathy, and a little grace someday, for something. I guess this quote falls into the category of Never Say Never.

JUNE 9

When you look at a field of dandelions, you can either see a hundred weeds or a hundred wishes.

I love this image. Can't you just see yourself blowing on a fluffy dandelion . . . launching dozens of dreams on a breeze?

JUNE 10

Ego says, "Once everything falls into place, I'll feel peace." Spirit says, "Find your peace, and then everything will fall into place."

— Marianne Williamson

Writer and speaker David Brooks gives a TED talk about the difference between what he calls résumé virtues and eulogy virtues. The first are accomplishments we'd list on a job application — distinctions we've achieved through ambition. The second virtues are the ways we've realized our inner callings and contributed to the betterment of others — all the meaningful stuff people share at a funeral. David says that these two sides of our nature are driven by very different forces. I guess you could call one force ego, and the other one spirit.

JUNE 11

It's the start of a brand-new day and I'm off like a herd of turtles.

Some days I find myself really dragging. I'll bet you do, too. Let's keep at it, though. At least we're moving forward!

JUNE 12

In spite of everything, I still believe that
people are really good at heart.
— ANNE FRANK

We're familiar with Annelies Marie Frank
— better known as Anne Frank — because
her father, Otto, published her diary and
other writings following World War II. This
loving thought from Anne is remarkable,
written inside the walls of a secret attic in
German-occupied Amsterdam where her
Jewish family hid for two years, terrified,
before being betrayed and sent to separate
death camps. Otto Frank was the only family member to survive, and was given Anne's
writings by the woman who'd helped hide
the family and saved Anne's diary and note-
books. In a letter to his mother, Otto wrote
of reading Anne's work: "There was revealed
a completely different Anne to the child that
I had lost. I had no idea of the depths of

her thoughts and feelings." In 1947, Otto published his daughter's words in the Netherlands under the title *Rear Annex.* Five years later, the book was published in the United States, titled *The Diary of a Young Girl.* Anne died at age fifteen, and would have turned ninety on this day in 2019.

A child can teach an adult three things: to be happy for no reason, to always be busy with something, and to know how to demand with all his might that which he desires.

— Paulo Coelho

Haley asks for what she wants. "Hold hands, Mommy."

might be filled with purple dinosaurs right now," Andy joked, "but he will hear the music play.

JUNE 14

Life is a cabaret, old chum.
— Fred Ebb, *Cabaret*

When I sat down with Andy Cohen, host of *Watch What Happens Live,* I wasn't sure why he chose lyrics from the musical *Cabaret* as one of his favorite quotes. I knew he loved music, but this one threw me. Quickly, I understood. "Come hear the music," Andy explained. "What are you doing inside? Live your life." He added that the quote also honors his late friend Natasha Richardson, who won the Tony Award for best actress in *Cabaret.* At late-night gatherings, he and friends would coax Natasha into singing the song, which she did, a cappella. "It was like a rallying cry for all of us," he said, "and it was absolutely the way she lived her life." Now the song will become a part of the soundtrack of his young son's life. "I'm ready to go to the cabaret with Benjamin. It might be filled with purple dinosaurs right now," Andy joked, "but he *will* hear the music play."

JUNE 15

There are all kinds of love in this world, but never the same love twice.
— F. Scott Fitzgerald

I believe this, which makes each and every love so unique and intimate and special. Just when I thought my heart couldn't possibly hold any more joy — that my love for Haley had filled it completely — Hope proved me wrong the second I laid eyes on her.

June 16

There is nothing in nature that blooms all year long, so don't expect yourself to do so either.

I'll take that as an invitation to chill out, hunker down, binge-watch, snuggle, snack, and wear soft pants whenever possible. With two little kids, though, that's really not happening! It used to look like this: I'd leave the phone downstairs, put on sweats, and grab a row of Ritz crackers. With the bedroom door shut, I'd pull down the blackout shades, get into bed, and binge-watch *The Real Housewives of . . .* anywhere, or some other mindless stuff. These days, I'd just feel guilty if I crawled into bed. "Mommy, where are you?" from the other side of the door is just too hard to resist.

June 17

I'm stuck between "I need to save money" and "You only live once."

There are so many of these choices!

"I shouldn't eat a whole tube of Pringles, but YOLO."

"I need sleep and shouldn't watch this movie, but YOLO."

"I should probably go through my stacks of crap, but YOLO."

(Fun fact: Movie star Zac Efron has "YOLO" tattooed on the side of his right hand.)

JUNE 18

Rules for happiness:
something to do, someone to love,
something to hope for.
— IMMANUEL KANT

I don't think we realize how simple it is and how little it takes to be happy; it's just not that complicated. That's why I love this quote so much. Surely to have at least *one* of these things is doable for each of us.

JUNE 19

I HATE MEN.
Never mind . . . he just texted back. False alarm.

Hahaha! Until next time . . .

June 20

Deep summer is when laziness finds respectability.

— Sam Keen

Look who's finally here! I'm in love with you, summer! Please consider taking longer to break up with me this year . . .

JUNE 21

My father gave me the greatest gift anyone could give another person, he believed in me.

— Jim Valvano

Dad's love and support — priceless. My father was the kind of guy who not only told us kids we could do anything we set our minds to, he showed us. When he and my mom moved to the United States from Egypt, they both completed college at Oklahoma University, where he also earned a PhD. He first worked at West Virginia University as a professor, teaching petroleum engineering, and then moved on to a job at the Department of Energy. When he left the government to start his own consulting company in Washington, DC, I remember being so proud reading "President" on his new business card. Your parents can give you all kinds of advice, but when you *watch* them practice what they preach, their words mean more. "Study hard," he'd say. "This is America . . . you can achieve things." Dad, you were so right. Thank you.

June 22

You are far too smart to be the only thing
standing in your way.
— Jennifer J. Freeman

There's a world full of people telling us
no . . . including ourselves. I think we can
talk ourselves out of something when we
haven't even tried step one. Bethenny Fran-
kel is someone who proved that *no one*
would stop her. I met her years ago on *Today*
during a segment about our emotional connections to food. Over the years, we've kept
in touch, and I've watched her create and
build the Skinnygirl brand. Her original idea
for a low-calorie margarita was genius, but
no one "got it." All the big liquor companies
turned her down. Publicists wouldn't go to
meetings with Bethenny because they didn't
take her idea seriously. Finally, a liquor
industry veteran shared her vision. He
became her business partner, and when

Skinnygirl hit the market, they couldn't keep up with demand. Way to go, Bethenny! Let's raise a glass to not standing in our own way today.

JUNE 23

Characterize people by their actions and you will never be fooled by their words.

All of us who've been cheated on are nodding our heads right now.

JUNE 24

There are some who bring a light so great to the world that even after they have gone the light remains.

When I posted this quote, many of the comments included the first and last names of people, people dearly missed. Boy, there's something so moving about declaring a name, willing it *in full* to be remembered and revered. Joel and I had a similar experience the other day when Haley asked us both the same question: "What's your daddy's name?" After we told her, and when we were alone, I asked Joel the last time he'd said his father's name out loud. He said it had been about fifteen years. This post reminded me how important it is to give voice to those we miss. Our voice.

JUNE 25

One day you will learn how to give and receive love like an open window and it will feel like summer every day.
— Sierra DeMulder

Pull back the curtain and push up that window, even if it's just an inch at a time.

JUNE 26

Patience is a form of wisdom. It demonstrates that we understand and accept the fact that sometimes things must unfold in their own time.

— Jon Kabat-Zinn

I'm not "wise" sometimes when it comes to small, daily frustrations like heavy traffic or snags in getting things done. Being impatient never solves anything, but still, I'll hit the "up" elevator button several times while I'm waiting! I do, though, like the concept of this one — try to breathe through the pain-in-the-neck stuff instead of fighting it.

JUNE 27

Fall in love with someone who doesn't
make you think love is hard.

When you've done the opposite, it's very
freeing when you finally fall for the right
person. With Joel, of course there are areas
to work on in our relationship, but by far,
the big-picture aspect of "us" is easy. And
that's amazing considering we met later in
life, when we both had established habits
and patterns. Still, we're meshing in a way
that works. I think one reason is that we
both know what matters in life; we're not
sweating the little stuff that we might have
in our twenties or thirties. I'm happy when
he comes home, I love that he kisses me
first and Haley and Hope witness that, I
love that he stands up from his chair whenever I get up from the table to get something. Life is easy with Joel, and I know how
very lucky that makes me.

JUNE 28

What you think, you become. What you feel, you attract. What you imagine, you create.

— Buddha

We have the power! It's the being-patient part that's hard . . . waiting, hoping for the results.

June 29

Enjoy the little things in life . . . because
one day you'll look back and realize they
were the big things.

— Kurt Vonnegut

Some of my favorites: sunrise, Joel's grilled
salmon, my mom's laughter, locking eyes
with Haley, Hope grabbing my finger, a run
through Central Park, a hot shower after a
long day.

June 30

Deep down, you already know the truth.

This one stings a bit. Maybe it hits a little too close to home. Maybe we're not ready to admit the truth to ourselves, whatever that "truth" may be. But remember, when a truth is buried deep within us, it's always there. So, which is harder . . . keeping it buried or digging it up?

JULY 1

Your speed doesn't matter, forward is forward.

Some say the early bird gets the worm. Others insist that slow and steady wins the race. Who's right? I say it's okay to be both the tortoise *and* the hare, depending on the day. What's your pace today?

JULY 2

In optimism there is magic. In pessimism there is nothing.

— Esther Hicks

I like the endless sparkle in that first -ism. I've been exposed to optimism my whole life because of my mom. I could share a thousand examples, but the beach comes to mind. If she's describing bad weather during a visit to Rehoboth, she'll say, "It was rainy, but you can't believe how much I needed a break from the sun." She's like that about everything, every day! If the weather forecast is bad for an upcoming trip, she's not having it. "Oh, please. They always say it's going to be cloudy until it's sunny." And you know what? My mom is usually right.

JULY 3

Fun is good.

— Dr. Seuss

And fun is just what the Dr. ordered! As we ease into the holiday, have you made your fun plans yet?

July 4

The true soldier fights not because he hates what is in front of him, but because he loves what is behind him.
— G. K. Chesterton

My favorite videos to post on the segment of *Today* we call "Morning Boost" involve military folks — veterans and active duty. I tear up every time we watch a seasoned veteran being honored or when a military member makes a surprise visit home. It's just *the best*. Please know that today and every day you are all loved and remembered. Thank you endlessly.

July 5

Life is better in flip-flops.

Yes! Be free, toes.

July 6

To me, you are perfect.
— *Love Actually*

Right around Valentine's Day 2016, I interviewed couples who — between them — had been married for more than 350 years. Incredible! They were so much fun, and very willing to share what they felt were a few secrets to their meaningful and long-lasting relationships. Here are a few to consider today:

1. One couple never goes to bed angry, even if she's left the bed for the couch. He just lies next to her on the living room floor. They realize that's ridiculous, and they end up back in bed, laughing.
2. One woman always says, "You're right, dear" (even though she *knows* he's wrong), and eventually, he

apologizes.

3. Another woman says she still sees her husband as the sexiest, most gorgeous man around. (To which he jokes, "Is she delusional, or what?")

July 7

It's your road, and yours alone. Others may walk it with you, but no one can walk it for you.

— Rumi

Make your plan, walk your walk, and link arms with the people who will make the journey more fun.

JULY 8

Grief, I've learned, is really just love. It's all the love you want to give but cannot. All of that unspent love gathers up in the corners of your eyes, the lump in your throat, and in that hollow part of your chest. Grief is just love with no place to go.

— Jamie Anderson

I posted this quote twice on Instagram. Both times, the comments were incredibly moving. People shared their losses — husbands, fathers, sisters. I feel like this quote somehow offers relief. Finally — in such a beautiful way — it makes sense of what's happening when we grieve.

JULY 9

Perhaps they are not stars in the sky, but rather openings where our loved ones shine down to let us know they are happy.
— Inuit proverb

. . . how I wonder how you are.

When my best friend Karen's husband, John, lost his mother, he told Karen that any dimes he found were a sign from his mom. Now, since Karen has lost John, she considers dimes a message of love from him.

JULY 10

My joy is nonnegotiable.
— Kathie Lee Gifford

Kathie Lee and I used to say this to each other — often in unison — when we worked together on the fourth hour of *Today*. We'd say it in the makeup room, on set, and sometimes on air. I'd never heard the phrase, and truly, Kath was the one who taught me the lesson behind it . . . the value of protecting joy. During our time together, I'd watch her say no to work or personal requests without a second thought. Not because she's lazy or uncaring — far from it. Instead, she explained that saying no to certain things was actually saying yes to herself, a way to honor her time for the projects and people she loves. As someone prone to spreading myself too thin, I consider her approach a good reminder. "Certain things are negotiable in life. I'll give a

249

little more time, I'll take a little less money, but joy — if you don't have joy in your life, what do you have?" says Kathie Lee. "Joy is where that soul of yours lives."

July 11

On particularly rough days when I'm sure
I can't possibly endure, I like to remind
myself that my track record for getting
through bad days so far is 100%. And
that's pretty good.

That's right! The numbers don't lie. Let's
keep this in mind today if things go south.

JULY 12

You live longer once you realize that any
time spent being unhappy is wasted.
— Ruth E. Renkl

Shoo, little black cloud! You're blocking my
happy.

July 13

Can we start the weekend over again? I wasn't ready.

Pretty please with a scrunchie on top?

On weekends, I still wake up around three a.m., but I let myself stay in bed until four thirty or five. Then our days are filled with awesomely mundane things. Joel and I have breakfast with the girls, and then we head off to Central Park. We bring along the bubble machine and colored chalk (so Haley can practice her *H*'s) and pass the hours hanging out and playing. Sometimes we visit the zoo, but always we have dinner at the City Diner. At six thirty, Joel and I will put the kids to bed, and then we fix mojitos. We snuggle on the couch and catch up . . . until it's lights-out for me at eight thirty. Aren't weekends the best?

July 14

If it's still in your mind, it is worth taking the risk.

— Paulo Coelho

In his book *The Second Mountain,* David Brooks tells the story of singer-songwriter Bruce Springsteen's realizing at seven years old that he wanted to be a performer. One night, Elvis Presley appeared on *The Ed Sullivan Show* and young Bruce — shy and awkward — was captivated by the free and fun way Elvis expressed himself. Scraping together money, his mother allowed Bruce to rent a guitar, but after a few weeks, he returned it, frustrated by his slow progress. Then, at fifteen, his passion sparked again when he saw the Beatles perform on *The Ed Sullivan Show.* This time, Bruce bought an old guitar, practiced relentlessly, and began performing anywhere and everywhere. Brooks uses the Boss to support advice he often shares with young people: Get to yourself quickly. If you know what you want to do, start doing it.

JULY 15

Quiet the mind, and the soul will speak.
— Ma Jaya Sati Bhagavati

At the start of 2017, Jenna Bush Hager and
I interviewed Agapi Stassinopoulos about
her new book, *Wake Up to the Joy of You,*
about meditation and self-care. She explained that we can use breathing tech-
niques to focus our minds. Before long, she
had the two of us relaxing, one hand on our
heart, the other on our belly. Our eyes were
closed and we were supposed to be imagin-
ing a waterfall, slowly inhaling and exhaling
as we did. Because I knew the floor director
would soon be prompting us to go to a commercial break, I opened my eyes a tiny bit
to check. When I saw what was airing, I
burst out laughing. Our director had put up
a live shot of the inside of the control room,
and everyone in it was pretending to meditate . . . eyes closed, hands correctly posed,

some slumped over in their chairs. Hilarious!

some slumped over in their chairs, Hilari oria!

July 16

No amount of guilt can change the past, and no amount of anxiety can change the future.

— Umar Ibn Al-Khattaab

We can certainly file this one under How Not to Waste Emotional Energy.

JULY 17

To plant a garden is to believe in tomorrow.

— Audrey Hepburn

It sure seems selfish, but I never really thought about the future very much until Haley and Hope came into my world. But now, with children — when I look at them — I see so far ahead and wonder what life will be like for them when I'm not around. Sometimes, when I look in their eyes, a little prayer bubbles up inside me. *God, please make this a beautiful world for them long after I'm gone.*

July 18

We tend to forget baby steps still move
us forward.

Progress is progress, baby!

When Haley was just a little more than a
year old, the two of us were in the living
room and she was testing out her world.
With one hand on the couch, she was
steadying herself so she could "walk." For
just a moment — maybe a step and a half
— she went hands-free. I can still picture
her doing it! My heart about exploded. I
was so proud of her! (Of course, when I
tried to get video of her doing it again, nothing.) I felt the same rush of joy when Hope
rolled over by herself for the first time.

JULY 19

I love that this morning's sunrise does not define itself by last night's sunset.
— Dr. Steve Maraboli

Another day, another opportunity. Sun + rise = a brand-new start. Go get 'em!

JULY 20

To forgive is to set a prisoner free and discover that the prisoner was you.
— Lewis Smedes

In 2015, a hate crime rocked both the nation and the Charleston, South Carolina, community that lost family and friends in a horrific attack. A twenty-one-year-old white man went on a shooting spree inside the Emanuel AME Church during an evening Bible study, murdering nine African Americans. Several years after the shooting, I sat down with three women who survived that day for a *Today* series called "Finding Forgiveness." Felicia Sanders, Polly Sheppard, and Jennifer Pinckney simply blew me away with their strength, grace, and faith. Felicia lost her son and an aunt; Jennifer's husband was killed. Still, they were determined — they *decided* — to forgive the shooter. "Sometimes I feel like I teeter-totter," Jennifer admitted, "but then I know the right thing to do is to forgive." Polly added this: "With forgiveness, you think you're letting someone else off the hook but you're actually letting yourself off the hook. If you keep the hate, there's no healing. We have to love each other."

JULY 21

Dear destiny, I am ready now.

Ya hear me? Alexa, play "Stronger" by Kelly Clarkson! Kelly is one of the most real, honest people I've ever met. I just *love* her. She's both hilarious and deep. One minute you're laughing your head off with her, the next you're weeping. If you've never listened to her song "Piece by Piece," I recommend it. The words are inspired by the pain she endured as a child when her father abandoned the family. Kelly wrote it for her husband, and for anyone who's been restored by love and loyalty.

July 22

Of this be sure: You do not find the happy life — you make it.

— Thomas S. Monson

Great news! We're in charge!

JULY 23

Worrying does not take away tomorrow's troubles. It takes away today's peace.

One of the many things I admire about Joel is that he doesn't worry. Instead, he takes care of business — when it's time to, and not before. Let's say he's got something he needs to address with a friend. I'll worry for him. "So, how are you going to do this? When will it happen?" Joel: "I'm just going to go there and talk to him." Same approach with work. If I know he's got an issue to deal with the next day, I'll ask him how he's doing. "I'm great," he'll say. And he is! Joel never lets tomorrow ruin his today.

July 24

What consumes your mind controls your life.

Goldie Hawn weighed in on this one when I posted it: *Right on baby!!!* Years ago, I went with Goldie and her son to an off-off-Broadway show. I had a wonderful time and enjoyed just being around them. I noticed that Goldie truly delights in the small things in life — the fact that her son was beside her, the big energy in such a small theater. Goldie's free-spirited, positive vibe is absolutely contagious, and she's the opposite of flighty — she's happy! Because she fills her life with causes that move her and people she loves, I totally understand why this quote resonated with Goldie.

July 25

Offline is the new luxury.

Oh, yes . . . please slather me with it.

When I left work for several months to bond with Hope, my world was drastically different, in the best way. I still used my phone, but mostly to order baby bottles or takeout food. The only breaking news I wanted to hear was that Hope had pooped. I remember my babysitter's saying one day, "I can't believe that helicopter crash in Manhattan." I said, "What crash?" I was so happy I didn't know. During that maternity leave, my mind was calmer, I slept better, and I just felt lighter. A break makes you realize how much noise is out there and how much stuff pretends to be a five-alarm fire when it's not. I've tried to remember how healthy it is — and how good it felt — to unplug for a while. I hope you can for a while today!

July 26

The emotion that can break your heart is sometimes the very one that heals it.
— Nicholas Sparks, *At First Sight*

This is so hard, isn't it? I guess it's a self-preservation thing. Who wants to feel yucky? Maybe that's why we need a partner in the process, like a song that makes us cry over and over again. Or a pen that captures feelings in a journal or in a letter we'll never send. The truth is, freedom may or *may not* be the payoff for putting ourselves through the wringer. I love the concept, but . . . *gulp.*

You are not just waiting in vain. There is a purpose behind every delay.
— Mandy Hale

When I filled out the papers for my first attempt at adoption, I remember the agency workers advising me to "wait wisely." When I asked what that meant, the explanation was basically this: *Try not to dwell. Live your life and know that there's a plan under way.* Because they know the immense emotions tied to children and the desire for them, they were giving me those two words to protect my heart and peace of mind. Thankfully, we were blessed with Haley very quickly, but the wait for Hope was a lot longer. I tried to tell myself to "wait wisely," but it was often hard. While it's true that . . . there *is* always a plan under way . . . it's still so hard to wait for our little angels, isn't it? For those of you still awaiting word, wondering, worrying . . . we feel you.

For those of you still awaiting word, wondering, worrying . . . we feel you.

July 28

Healing doesn't mean the damage never existed. It means the damage no longer controls your life.

— Akshay Dubey

In 2016, I was lucky enough to share in a surprise with the Held family. Our goal was to honor Les Held — beloved husband, father, and survivor. When he was six, Les and his family were taken to a Nazi concentration camp. Miraculously, on the day Les was sent to the gas chamber, the gas supply ran dry. When he was brought before a firing squad, an old man pushed him down and took a bullet for him. Later, Les made his way to America and started a family. "My father's philosophy on life is optimism and happiness," his son, Aaron, told me. "Given his background, that's what's so surprising." Because Les is a huge fan of tennis — and superstar John McEnroe —

his family joined with *Today* to arrange a surprise meeting at the US Open. Les thought he was simply enjoying John's Legends Match until he saw himself on the jumbotron! Following a big hug, John and Les took to the court for a few volleys. The big smile on Les's face was no surprise. This positive, resilient man is always wearing one.

The real gift of gratitude is that the more grateful you are, the more present you become.

— Robert Holden

When I visited Uniondale High School in New York, students couldn't help but sing the praises of their choir director, Lynette Carr-Hicks. "I got kicked out of one school, had some suspensions," Emmanuel Beauge told me, "but this choir changed me." After school, choir members train with Lynette until ten o'clock at night, honing both their physical and vocal fitness. The atmosphere is fun and safe, and Lynette — whom the kids call Mom — demands excellence. "I guess it's because I get on them like a mother," she said, laughing. "Take that hat off your head! Pull up those pants!" Rhythm of the Knight is not just a show choir, it's a training ground for the future. Every member graduates and goes to college. In 2018, Lynette and her choir fulfilled their goal of being the best. Together, they were named grand champions at Show Choir Nationals. The only thing bigger than the trophy they won was their collective pride and gratitude. "I was walking down the hallway," Jasmine McKay said, "and I was like, *Wait a minute . . . we just did this!*"

JULY 30

It always seems impossible until it's done.
— NELSON MANDELA

Susan B. Anthony. Neil Armstrong. Steve Jobs. Moana.

Love is not "if" or "because." Love is "anyway" and "even though" and "in spite of."

Unconditional love! It's never a choice, it just is. When I think of the way we feel about our kids and our pets, *that* kind of love is the most pure.

AUGUST 1

If you see something beautiful in someone, speak it.

— Ruthie Lindsey

I left a charity event in New York City years ago with a phrase I love and use to this day. Former president Bill Clinton was the keynote speaker and devoted part of his speech to the word *"sawubona,"* a South African Zulu greeting that means "I see you." Afterward, I thought about the statement, profound in its simplicity and intimacy. "I see you." On a deeper level, "I see your personality. I see your essence." When I share those three words with my nieces, they'll ask, "Why do you say that, Aunt Hodie?" I try to explain to them how much I value their little spirits, their everything. I say it to Haley, Hope, and other babies, too. "I see you." I'm here with you. Recently, I read a bit more on *sawubona* and I love this part of the story: the greeting is exchanged in small African villages where everyone knows one another and has for years. To me, that's so refreshing and compelling. *Hey, we cross paths all the time, but still . . . I see you.*

August 2

Sometimes I shock myself with the smart stuff I say and do. Then, there are times when I try to get out of the car with my seat belt on.

Or when I realize I've had my shirt on backwards all day.

AUGUST 3

The most important thing in life is to stop
saying "I wish" and start saying "I will."
— CHARLES DICKENS

When my mother was sixty years old, she
vowed to run in and finish the Marine
Corps Marathon in Washington, DC. At the
start of the race, Hala, Adel, and I cheered
her on and mapped out places along the
route where we'd be able to yell to her as
she churned through the miles. My mom
was doing great until mile 10, when she
began to struggle. "Mom needs support!"
Hala announced. I was the only one of us
three wearing sneakers, so I jumped in
beside my mom. We talked as we ran, and
kept a lookout for Adel and Hala. A big
burst of adrenaline kicked in when we realized that if we didn't hit a certain land-
mark at a specified time, we'd be required
to leave the course and take a bus. No way!

Somehow we found the will to pick up the pace. At the finish line, I stopped short so I could watch my mom cross it all by herself. Her amazing, determined self.

August 4

I Googled my symptoms. Turns out I just needed to go to the beach.

Sun, surf, sand. The *best* medicine.

August 5

It's a lot easier to be angry at someone than it is to tell them you're hurt.

— Tom Gates

He's right. But sometimes you don't have time for a whole "I'm hurt" conversation. So you don't have it. And then later, you end up exploding like a raging maniac. Yeah, okay. You're right, Mr. Gates.

August 6

We all have two lives. The second one starts when we realize we only have one.
— Confucius

If only this could happen without all the scary stuff, but sometimes that's what it takes.

August 7

Nothing ever goes away until it has
taught us what we need to know.
— PEMA CHÖDRÖN

And I guess we have to be willing to learn,
too.

AUGUST 8

A mother is a person who, seeing there are only four pieces of pie for five people, promptly announces she never did care for pie.

— Tenneva Jordan

Change "pie" to "baklava" and yep, that's my mom.

Don't look back. You're not going that way.

During my journey through breast cancer, I wrote the word "FORWARD" at the bottom of every journal page. "FORWARD." The last word on every page. That indicated to me that I wasn't stuck. I wasn't going to live in this place forever . . . just right now. It's amazing how much power one word can have, isn't it? So, when the producers at NBC laid eyes on those pink cancer-awareness bracelets, they thought, *Why not put "FORWARD" on a ring?* What a genius idea! Now whenever I'm wearing one and someone shares their cancer journey with me, I'll give the ring to them and replace it with another. Other people do that, too: wear it, then give it away. It's a pass-it-on thing. FORWARD. Today may be a good day to think about facing that way.

August 10

One moment can change a day, one day
can change a life, and one life can
change the world.

— Buddha

I love the way these words celebrate the power of one. It's easy to think change requires *team transformation*! But sometimes nothing more is needed than a singular something — or someone — to generate momentum and change the course of life.

AUGUST 11

I may not be your first date, your first kiss, or your first love; I just want to be your last everything.

Joel texted this to me. *Swooooon . . .*

AUGUST 12

Pick the weeds and keep the flowers.
— Calamity McEntire

Songwriters like Kelly Clarkson are word-smiths, and it was these seven words that moved her one day. Kelly was talking with her friend Calamity about frustrations in her life and the people who were creating them. "Pick the weeds and keep the flowers," Calamity suggested. Kelly says the phrase hit home: sometimes you're simply not on the same path with someone anymore and you have to part ways with them. It can be difficult, but Kelly says it's important to pull people close who make you a better person and clear out the ones who are negative. "There are people who are great humans," she says, "they're just not great for me."

Accept both compliments and criticism. It takes both sun and rain for a flower to grow.

True, but nowadays we should consider the source.

August 14

In seeking happiness for others, you will find it in yourself.

I'm picturing me pushing Haley on a swing at the playground. She's squealing, I'm smiling. No telling who's happier!

August 15

The privilege of a lifetime is being who you are.

— Joseph Campbell

Sometimes it takes a while to figure out who you are professionally, but who you are as a person is nothing to overthink. Just be you!

AUGUST 16

There is an instinct in a woman to love most her own child; and an instinct to make any child who needs her love, her own.

— Robert Brault

I took a little trip back in time the other day. Because of this book, I was leafing through one of my previous books, *Where We Belong,* and happened upon my thoughts in 2016: "I've known for a long time where I belong, and yet I'm on the slow track to arriving there. I belong with kids, little kids who need guidance and love. That plan, well, had some snags — divorce, illness, and now, my age. Still, I'll get there . . . to the place where what brings me the most joy brings joy to others, too." At the time, I thought perhaps that place was a summer camp for underprivileged kids. Boy, life is so incredible, isn't it? Just one year later, I'd found the courage to dream even bigger, and thankfully, raising my daughters — Hope and Haley — is my greatest joy.

August 17

If you don't like something, just take away
its only power: your attention.

Doesn't it feel like there are so many things screaming at us? "Look at me! I'm right here on your phone! Look at me!" You feel a buzz and you want to look. Sometimes it's a news alert, sometimes it's a text or email, begging for attention. Well, enough! I think we have to give our eyes and minds a break. At work, I can't, for obvious reasons. But on my own time, I try to filter things out. What deserves my time and my thoughts? I've gotten out of the habit of looking at my Twitter or news feed every ten seconds, because what's trending is probably something not so great. Instead, I might flip on *Love It or List It* or a Chip and Joanna show, or I'll listen to music. We often have Neil Diamond playing on Pandora because you can sing along to every song.

I'm not saying be oblivious to the world, but be judicious. Decide that your brain *will not* be exposed to crap 24/7. We can't control the world, but we can protect our little corner of it.

The human spirit is stronger than anything that can happen to it.

— C. C. Scott

The term "human spirit" is hard to define, isn't it? Certainly it's a winning combination of qualities that *will us* to keep moving forward: hope, purpose, faith, love, gratitude.

AUGUST 19

When it is all finished, you will discover it was never random.

Life circled back on me one day when I happened upon a journal entry I'd written years earlier. In 2014, on a flight to Florida, a woman took the center seat as I sat by the window. As other passengers boarded, she told me that she was going to say something and I might think she was crazy. "Okay," I said. She told me that my dad was there and watching over me. I just looked at her, stunned. Then she told me he would be a great help to me on an upcoming project. Back then, I assumed the project might involve work or perhaps a big trip. But in 2017, "The Project" was my code name for the process of adopting a baby. *Dad!* When I reread the journal entry about my conversation on that flight, my body was numb and sizzling with goose bumps at the same time. I've always marveled at how smoothly everything unfolded with Haley, as if there was a guiding hand involved. Now, thanks to the words of the woman in the middle seat, I truly believe there was.

AUGUST 20

Stop yourself from stopping yourself.

During my 2019 interview with Lindsey Vonn, the most successful female ski racer of all time, she showed me a tattoo on the inside of her left ring finger. The inked image is a shark, which she said she chose for two reasons. "Sharks go after what they want," she explained, "and they always keep moving forward." Lindsey's drive and grit has always amazed me. When most of us sustain a serious injury, we shy away from whatever caused it. Not Lindsey. Somehow, after jarred spinal joints, knee surgeries, a fractured arm and ankle — and the list goes on — she did the physical and mental work to keep getting back on her skis, not only returning to high-level competition but prevailing, a stunning eighty-two wins to her name. Lindsay told me that except for insects and other creepy crawlies, she's not afraid of anything, including the inevitable falls on the slopes and in life. "Pick yourself back up. Tomorrow's a new day, a new opportunity. Don't let your past hold you back."

August 21

Dear Friday, I'm so glad we are back together. I'm sorry you had to see me with Monday — Thursday, but I swear I was thinking of you the whole time.

Signed, Everyone.

AUGUST 22

They tried to bury us. They didn't know we
were seeds.

— Dinos Christianopoulos

Ooooh . . . can't you just see those tiny
green sprouts peeking up from the dirt? I
love the comeback-kid spirit of this one.

August 23

If ever there is a tomorrow when we're not together, there is something you must always remember. You are braver than you believe, stronger than you seem, and smarter than you think. But the most important thing is, even if we're apart . . . I'll always be with you.
— *Pooh's Grand Adventure*

Gosh, this fills me up and crushes me at the same time. There is comfort in knowing the ones we love are always with us, but I don't want the "apart" time.

AUGUST 24

Trust yourself. You've survived a lot, and you'll survive whatever is coming.

— Robert Tew

We really do tend to forget how much we've been through, maybe to protect our peace of mind. This message is a great reminder to take a peek once in a while at your Survivor Seal of Approval.

AUGUST 25

Let's stop the glorification of busy.
— Guy Kawasaki

I feel like this one needs a hashtag or a flag or a ribbon or something! Just because we're doing *something* doesn't necessarily mean we're doing something *important.* I remember as a freshman on the high school basketball team, I would run around the court like a crazy person. I had no idea what I was doing, so I just went all out. But as a sophomore, I learned when to sprint and when to pause. And you know what? I was a much better player when I expended energy more wisely. Now that I have kids, I'm still busy, but I know I'm using my time more efficiently than ever. Or maybe doing mom things just feels more fulfilling. Either way, it's probably a good idea to replace busy with lazy from time to time and feel fine about it. Maybe today?

You are perfect exactly as you are. There is no need to change anything except the thoughts that you are not good enough.

Don't let negative thoughts run the show today!

Repeat after me:
It is not my responsibility to heal, save,
punish, or control other people.

Whoever *me* is, I'll bet she does yoga, eats clean, and is a very content person.

August 28

Life is what happens between coffee and
wine.

I might slip another coffee in there around
two o'clock in the afternoon . . .

Happiness is your nature. It is not wrong to desire it. What is wrong is seeking it outside when it is inside.

— Sri Ramana Maharshi

I heard a conversation the other day about how we're *born* happy. Think of little kids, who giggle and play all day. Even puppies and kittens are full of energy and a willingness to engage with everyone. Happiness is part of us! If we remember that, maybe we'll lose less of it as we move through our days.

August 30

The wound is the place where the light enters you.

— Rumi

After comedienne Joan Rivers died, her daughter, Melissa, wrote a book about her mother titled *The Book of Joan.* In front of a large audience at the 92nd Street Y, I was about to begin interviewing Melissa about the book and her mom. Before I began, though, I did what my friend Larry Flick suggested. (Larry is a talk and music host on SiriusXM radio, and an incredibly insightful person.) Larry said, "Bring up the lights and ask everyone in the audience who's lost a parent." So I did. Literally, almost every hand went up. Then I asked, "Who's afraid of losing a parent?" The rest of the hands went up. Now Melissa knew she was talking to people who would relate to her pain. We all exhaled and began the evening together. I know they say misery loves company, but perhaps the deeper bond between us is that vulnerability loves company.

AUGUST 31

A strong woman looks a challenge dead in the eye and gives it a wink.

— Gina Carey

And maybe even some "bring it" fingers.

Choose hope.

I sure did, but with a capital letter. When Joel and I agreed that we wanted to open our lives to the possibility of another child, only one name would do for a daughter: Hope. Honestly, there was no debate. There was no "Let's pick from three names." Our baby would be that word personified. After all, that's what we'd be doing and feeling as we waited. Then, a year and a half later, word came that a baby girl was ours. *We're coming, Hope.* When I first laid eyes on her, I knew the name was exactly right! The choice of her middle name was easy, too: Catherine, after my best friend Karen's daughter, a young girl who lost her beloved father to cancer. I'd love it if Catherine's quiet strength develops within Hope, too. I'm still amazed and grateful that after all the wishing and waiting, hope paved the way for pure happiness . . . and Hope.

September 2

Your mind will always believe everything you tell it. Feed it faith. Feed it truth. Feed it with love.

I totally believe this. Doesn't mean it's easy, though. One of my favorite authors, Anne Lamott, talks about the bad stuff we feed our brains. In her book *Bird by Bird*, she refers to the noise in our heads as "radio station KFKD." Those call letters say it all. We can mentally beat ourselves up 24/7 *or* we can block that station. Let's tune in — as often as we can — to KLUV instead.

I love it when someone's laugh is funnier
than the joke.

Isn't laughing the best? This makes me think
of my dear friend Janie. I love hearing her
laugh because it means one of us has made
the other bust up yet again. Jane and I have
a decades-old history of sharing the kind of
laughter that makes you gasp for air, cry,
and slap the table. I gotta say, of all the feelings on planet Earth, laughing like a lunatic
has got to be one of the best. For all the
times you've made me spit out whatever I'm
drinking, Janie, thank you.

Sometimes when you wonder why you can't hear God's voice during your trials, remember the teacher is always quiet during the test.

This is comforting, especially when we feel so alone.

SEPTEMBER 5

The greatest mistake you can make in life is to be continually fearing you will make one.

— Elbert Hubbard

If only there were spell-check for daily life, too — so we'd just go for it, knowing any potential mistakes would be autocorrected!

September 6

The cure for anything is salt water: sweat, tears, or the sea.

— Isak Dinesen

I remember running along the Mississippi River a lot when I finally decided to leave New Orleans for New York City. Even though I'd moved around a lot for work, I knew relocating this time would crush me. Leaving behind New Orleans and its people hit me like a breakup. All those miles along the river helped me process my mixed emotions. Maybe you feel this way too — there's just something soothing about working through pain alongside water. Maybe it's the constant motion, the moving forward . . . something we can always rely on to be there for us as we heal.

September 7

Breathe, darling. This is just a chapter. It's not your whole story.

— S. C. Lourie

This reminds me of the city of New Orleans. After the horror of Hurricane Katrina unfolded and the water began to subside, I'd often be asked at speaking engagements how the city was faring. "How are they doin'?" people would ask, their eyes sad. I would take a breath and ask a question right back. "Have you ever met anybody from New Orleans?" I'd stiffen my spine a bit and say, "They are back-straight people. They are get-up-off-your-knees people. That's how they're doing." Look, I knew everyone was sincere, but I guess I just wanted people to see beyond those awful images that were seared into the nation's psyche. Yes, it happened, but Katrina is *not*

New Orleans's whole story. Take a trip to the Big Easy and find out for yourself!

SEPTEMBER 8

What lies behind us and what lies before us are tiny matters compared to what lies within us.

— Ralph Waldo Emerson

If Maria Shriver's talking, I'm listening. I've learned so much from her about navigating life. Maria told me she loves this Emerson quote because it offers her relief and comfort in knowing that we don't have to be afraid; everything we need to handle our challenges is within us. She says, "Anything you think you're missing, you're wrong. It's in you. You can call that faith in yourself or a higher power, but you've got it. The sooner you know that, the more wild and free and authentic your life will be."

Be kind, for everyone you meet is fighting
a battle you know nothing about.
— WENDY MASS

It's easy to forget how much is going on for
people as they navigate their day . . . at
work, in traffic, on a plane. Being kind to
someone who's acting poorly can be hard,
but maybe they're just losing the battle in
that moment. I bet we'll run into one — or
five — people today who are fighting a silent
battle.

SEPTEMBER 10

Happiness is available. Please help yourself to it.

— Thich Nhat Hanh

Years ago, my *Today* show colleague Al Roker and I were covering Mardi Gras in New Orleans, and by the time we flew back to New York City and drove home, it was about two o'clock in the morning. There was just enough time to shower and get to work — bleary eyed — by four a.m. When I arrived, I heard someone singing . . . loudly. Turns out, it was Al! I couldn't believe it. I asked him, "How come you're always in a good mood, Al?" Wearing that signature smile of his, he said, "Because my dad drove a city bus and I get to come to 30 Rock every day." (More singing.) That's Al in a nutshell. Happiness truly *is* available.

The broken will always be able to love harder than most. Once you've been in the dark, you learn to appreciate everything that shines.

— Zachry K. Douglas

In May 2016, I was honored to deliver the commencement speech for Tulane University. During my talk, I shared a list of ten lessons the graduates might one day find helpful. When I got to number nine, I pointed to a man in the crowd who I'd met in New Orleans two decades earlier. "Lesson number nine is sitting right here in front of me." I briefly shared the story of Derrick Edwards, who became a quadriplegic following a high school football injury yet still pursued his dreams. "Derrick Edwards graduated high school," I told the crowd, as Derrick's face was featured on the jumbotron. I explained that he also earned two college degrees plus a law degree. His proud mother beamed beside her son. "And do you know what Derrick Edwards is doing today? Derrick Edwards, in the front row, is running for US Senate." The crowd exploded and I smiled at Derrick. "Lesson number nine."

SEPTEMBER 12

Sometimes life doesn't give you something
you want — not because you don't deserve it, but because you deserve more.

Life is so pesky that way. Only in hindsight
do we realize everything happened for a
reason. (Except for all that stuff that makes
absolutely no sense . . .)

SEPTEMBER 13

Three minutes of music, years of memories.

Music is memory's time capsule: where you were, who you were with, what you were doing, how a song made you feel so long ago. What song instantly transports you back in time?

September 14

It's hard to beat a person who never gives up.

— Babe Ruth

If you're tired, if you're frustrated, if you're hopeless, if you're lost, if you're confused . . . keep going.

SEPTEMBER 15

When looking back doesn't interest you anymore, you're doing something right.

I had this experience recently . . . a breakthrough that snuck up on me. I won't give the person much ink, but guess what? Nothing you do matters to me anymore. I'm free.

It's time to rest. Everything is going to be
okay.

Doesn't this just sound so good? *Sigh . . .*

September 17

You were born to be real, not to be perfect.
— Ralph Marston

To be perfectly real! NBA superstar and sports analyst Shaquille O'Neal told me a great story in 2019 about his mother and the day she told him to keep it real. Shaq said that when he first started using Twitter, he was in "show-off" mode, posting photos of himself and his fancy belongings. "Look at my house . . . look at my boat," he said, describing his flashy Twitter feed. One day, Shaq's mother called him on the phone. "She said, 'Stop showing off. Be humble.' " Immediately, Shaq developed a new plan for Twitter: 60 percent of a post should entertain, 30 percent should inspire, and 10 percent should inform. "My mom's never been wrong," Shaq said, "and she's always so calm about her approach." Throughout his life, Shaq said his mother has always been spot-on with her advice. Sitting there with this seven-foot-one, three-hundred-plus-pound man, listening to him talk so lovingly about his mom was very dear — and very real.

September 18

Never suppress a generous thought.
— Camilla E. Kimball

Pop that thought bubble and free your kindness! Someone will be grateful you did.

SEPTEMBER 19

It is not too late. You are not too old. You are right on time — and you are better than you know.
— MARIANNE WILLIAMSON

When I was going through the mental gymnastics of adopting a baby — at fifty-two — I immediately thought of Sandra Bullock. I knew that she'd adopted her son, on her own, just several years shy of age fifty, and then her daughter five years later. How cool! I'd met Sandra on the set of *Today* and loved her, so I decided to reach out to her agent about "a private matter." Sandra immediately called me. From the minute we started talking, my heart just sang. She told me I was about to go on the greatest adventure of my life. We also talked a lot about the nuts and bolts of adopting, but mostly she was a fantastic cheerleader for the idea. She said of all the things she'd

338

done in her life, adopting trumped them all . . . it wasn't even close. After talking with Sandra, my confidence and excitement soared! Thanks for the inspiration, friend. I'll always remember this text from you: "Get ready to fall in love like you've never fallen before."

SEPTEMBER 20

Life is not a fairy-tale. If you lose your shoe at midnight, you're drunk.

My girl Savannah Guthrie posted this on Instagram: *Don't judge* . . .

September 21

The world is changed by your example,
not by your opinion.

— Paulo Coelho

Fist bump, Paulo. These days there's no
shortage of platforms for opinions: social
media, websites, broadcast channels. More
than ever it's important to consider that
working on ourselves instead of our key-
boards is the most effective — and respect-
ful — approach.

When you talk, you are only repeating what you already know. But if you listen, you may learn something new.

— The Dalai Lama

It's that old adage about why God gave us one mouth and two ears.

I love the 3 a.m. version of people. Vulnerable. Honest. Real.

Because I'm someone who gets up before dawn, I feel a connection with my fellow early birds at work. There seems to be a vulnerability to people at that hour. Maybe we're tired and there aren't as many mental filters, so we just tell it like it is. Sometimes the makeup room feels like a confessional. I truly love New York City's constant energy, but there's just a special vibe in those wee morning hours.

SEPTEMBER 24

Memories made at the beach last a
lifetime.

Some of my favorite photos are the ones
snapped at the beach. I have so many,
stretching across generations. I love the old
ones where our family of five is standing in
the bubbling surf, all different heights and
in different suits, wearing the same ear-to-
ear smiles. My mom, my siblings, and I still
vacation at the beach, our photos now
featuring nieces frolicking on the sand and
in the sea. When Haley was just a baby,
wearing a floppy hat and pink bathing suit,
I dipped her toes in the pool. I couldn't
wait! Our first trip to the beach together
thrilled me, and I'm so excited to make endless memories with her and Hope by the
shore. Joel loves the beach, too, and so many
of my favorite memories involve watching

the sun dip behind the ocean with him by
my side.

September 25

Knowing what you need to do to improve your life takes wisdom. Pushing yourself to do it takes courage.

— Mel Robbins

Usually, too, we think, *Why didn't I do this a long time ago!* once we finally find the courage.

SEPTEMBER 26

And so the adventure begins.

I posted this on April 8, 2018, the very first morning Jenna Bush Hager joined me as co-host of the fourth hour of *Today.* Because Jenna's energy and enthusiasm have been contagious since the moment I met her, there was no doubt in my mind that we were beginning an adventure together. From the sparkle in her eye to the pep in her step as we walked to the set, I knew Jenna's first day in her new role felt like the first day of school, times a thousand. Within the first few minutes she was crying (and laughing at herself crying), overwhelmed by this exciting next chapter in her career. More tears flowed during heartfelt video messages from her parents — former president George W. Bush and first lady Laura Bush — and her twin sister, Barbara. The dam fully broke when her sweet husband, Henry, and beautiful daughters, Mila and Poppy, surprised her, complete with a bouquet of red roses. Even before that special welcome to the show, I got the sense that Jenna knew she was the puzzle piece we were looking for . . . and you know what? She is.

book (and [other books]) to my girls. It
makes me so happy.

SEPTEMBER 27

I feel like a part of my soul has loved you
since the beginning of everything. Maybe
we're from the same star.
— Emery Allen

I've loved you since forever! That sweet
sentiment became the title of my first
children's book because of a conversation I
had with a wonderful writer named Margaret and her colleagues at HarperCollins.
At our meeting, I mentioned that during
my wait for Haley, I scribbled "I've loved
you since forever" on nearly every page of
my journal. I explained that I could feel
her . . . almost physically . . . before I even
met her. My love for her was without a
beginning or an end; it was just there,
always. Those five words became both our
title and the inspiration for the story. Suzie
Mason's beautiful illustrations brought
everything to life. Every time I read the

book (and lots of books!) to my girls, it makes me so happy.

SEPTEMBER 28

Doubt kills more dreams than failure ever will.
                                    — SUZY KASSEM

The older I get, the more I dismiss doubt, but that doesn't mean it's completely moved out of my being. Doubt stinks. It darts around the mind like an eraser, trying to rub out a dream when it sees one forming. I like the message here — that we may try and fail, but at least we're actively chasing our dreams.

September 29

A beautiful face will age and a perfect body will change, but a beautiful soul will always be a beautiful soul.

Loving this.

September 30

I love hanging out with people who make me forget to look at my phone.

It's crazy how addicted we are (perhaps not you) to our phones. They are our everything, plying us with endless information and entertainment. How refreshing when someone miraculously breaks that dysfunctional bond . . . when the spell cast by a screen is completely broken by a human being.

OCTOBER 1

We either make ourselves miserable or we make ourselves strong. The amount of work is the same.

— Carlos Castaneda

Seems like a no-brainer when it's served up like this, right?

OCTOBER 2

Attention is the rarest and purest form of generosity.

— Simone Weil

I see this two ways:

1. In this world of so many distractions, paying attention to someone is absolutely a conscious choice we make.
2. To pay someone attention is to be with them in the moment, focusing on what they need and what makes them happy.

OCTOBER 3

The adult version of "Head, shoulders, knees, and toes" is "Wallet, glasses, keys, and phone."

Ha! I will think of this every time we act out this song in Haley's play group.

OCTOBER 4

When was the last time you did
something for the first time?

I gotta say, Joel is the best at this. I could offer a dozen examples, but several come to mind: he and I are taking guitar lessons together, at fifty-eight he learned how to ice-skate so he could play on a hockey team, he agreed to become Haley's dad at fifty-nine, and he welcomed Hope and deliberately switched jobs at nearly sixty-one. As we get older, "first times" seem to dwindle. Unless you're Joel.

OCTOBER 5

Don't underestimate the healing power of these three things: music, the ocean, and the stars.

All three at the same time is perfection!

OCTOBER 6

Pay attention to the things you are naturally drawn to. They are often connected to your path, passion, and purpose in life. Have the courage to follow them.

— Ruben Chavez

For more than fifteen years, my friend and *Today* colleague Maria Shriver has courageously fought to eradicate Alzheimer's, a passion that sparked because she paid extra attention to something that was right in front of her. When her father, Sargent Shriver, developed Alzheimer's disease, Maria discovered that more than twice as many women suffer from the ailment as men. Some studies indicate it's because women tend to live longer, but Maria thought other pieces of the puzzle must be missing. Not only were millions of women suffering from Alzheimer's, they were also the main caregivers for family members stricken with the disease. As a female and a former caregiver to her father, Maria was compelled to start the Women's Alzheimer's Movement, a nonprofit organization dedicated to raising awareness about the disease, funding research for a cure, and developing support for women. Her annual Move for Minds initiative promotes disease prevention through diet, exercise, and ample sleep. Talk about paying attention — way to go, Maria!

OCTOBER 7

The secret of your future is hidden in your daily routine.

— Mike Murdock

This reminds me of an Annie Dillard quote: "The way you live your days is the way you live your life." I've tried to tackle exercise this way . . . to do a little a lot. If every day you get your heart rate up, all of a sudden you've got yourself a daily routine!

OCTOBER 8

"You're still a rock star," I whisper to myself as I take my multivitamin and climb in bed at 9:45.

Nine forty-five? You *are* a rock star! On weekdays (and most weekends . . . sorry, Joel!), I go to bed by eight o'clock. Really, once I put the kids down, I go down. It's over. That three fifteen a.m. alarm's a-comin'! As my bedtimes grew earlier and earlier, I think at first Joel was in shock: "Huh? Right now?" Poor Joel. "I thought we were going to watch *Billions.*" Nope. Lights-out for me. I know there are shows on television after eight p.m., but I've never seen them. In fact, a whole world goes on without me. But that's okay. Lots of good stuff happens before even the sun decides to wake up.

OCTOBER 9

The two most important days in your life are the day you were born . . . and the day you find out why.

— Ernest T. Campbell

In the first months after I brought Haley home, no one but my inner circle knew I'd adopted a baby. One day, as I walked by myself toward Duane Reade for something, a woman said hello and asked me the question that for so long had required a no from me. She asked, "Do you have kids?" There it was. The kid question. My entire adult life I'd shaken my head no, though I'd beamed with pride as I spoke about my nieces. But this time, I got to picture a beautiful face and deep brown eyes. I smiled at the woman ear to ear. With gratitude and excitement and love (and with my heart bursting), I answered, "Yes. I have a daughter. Her name is Haley Joy." Those magic words finally came out of my mouth and danced around my ears. *Yes, I do!* In those few seconds, my dream-come-true found its voice.

OCTOBER 10

You never know how strong you are until being strong is the only choice you have.
— Bob Marley

Boy, so true. One fateful day, you realize that even though fear and weakness are jumping up and down yelling, "Choose me!" strength is the only thing that has your back.

OCTOBER 11

Sometimes a moment of quiet is all you
need.

For me, airplanes are one place to chill.
Hoodie up, earbuds in, playlist on shuffle.
Daily, though, my favorite "me time" is
waking up at three fifteen. I light a candle,
put on music, and write in my journal (and
select a quote!). Sacrificing an extra half
hour of sleep is not how I see it. That time
by myself is so restorative and calming. I
guess it's my way of creating a solid foundation for whatever the day asks of me. Can
you carve out a moment of quiet today?

OCTOBER 12

I can and I will. Watch me.

Yes! Is that Rachel Platten's "Fight Song" I hear?

OCTOBER 13

Sometimes you have to stop being scared and go for it. Either it will work or it won't. That's life.

The simplicity of this is helpful, isn't it? No gray area, no big deal. Do your thing and move on.

OCTOBER 14

Stop looking for happiness in the same place you lost it.

Why do we do that? On a simpler level, it's like eating an entire sleeve of Thin Mints, enjoying it, regretting it, and then doing it again.

OCTOBER 15

Sometimes you need to talk to a two-year-old so you can understand life again.

One afternoon, Haley walked into the playroom we visit often, opened her arms to four strangers, and said, "Group hug!" And you know what? All four were *all* in. Two grandparents and two parents got up off a bench and wrapped her up in their arms. It was one of the best things I've ever seen! A two-year-old reminded me how pure and natural it is to ask for love. I don't know why, but it's easy — at least for me — to forget sometimes just to ask for what I need.

OCTOBER 16

Sometimes the best thing you can do is
to not think, not wonder, not imagine, and
not obsess. Just breathe, and have faith
that everything will work out for the best.

A month after posting this quote, I received
the kindest letter from a young woman
named Ali. She'd been diagnosed with a
golf-ball-sized brain tumor, which was steal-
ing her sight in one eye. Following a fully
successful surgery — and with perfect
eyesight — Ali penned me a note, the
stationery topped with an embossed gold
butterfly. It reads in part, "Your daily Instagram posts brought me so much peace in
the days following my diagnosis. I will
always remember the morning of January
6th waking up in the darkest of dark and
then reading this post from you. I smiled, I
sobbed, I hung onto those words and never
looked back in the dark again. Thank you

for proving to me that having faith is the easy part. This life is so amazing and miracles are real!" Wow, Ali. I love your spirit! You're like that little gold butterfly, taking flight and inspiring us all with your lightness of being.

OCTOBER 17

Go find yourself first so you can also find me.

— Rumi

What a cool request. Please bring me your best self. I'm waiting . . .

OCTOBER 18

May you take comfort in knowing an angel is watching over you.

I posted an image of a jar of pennies along with the phrase "Pennies from Heaven" after a woman called in to my Sirius radio show during a segment we call "Play It Forward." The idea is for listeners to share stories celebrating people who did something kind for them, and then we play a song that connects to the vibe of the story. I'll never forget a call from "Carrie from Texas," who said she worked as an elementary school teacher. She explained that her child had been sick and died and that whenever she found a penny, she took it as a sign from her son, Ryan, a feeling she'd shared with her students. Carrie explained that when pennies kept turning up at school, she discovered that a little boy had raided his piggy bank and placed pennies around school for her to find. How utterly dear! When I posted the jar image the next morning, so many people commented on the power of pennies in their own lives, copper touchstones sent by angels.

OCTOBER 19

The happiness in your life depends upon the quality of your thoughts.

— Marcus Aurelius

I've journaled for decades, so adding daily entries about gratitude felt doable to me. Several years ago, I learned about the idea watching a TED talk I happened upon at the gym. Psychologist Shawn Achor explained in the video that we can reprogram our brains by incorporating daily habits like writing down people or experiences we're grateful for. *Why not give it a shot?* I thought. Turns out, it was easy and pleasing, and now I always feel a bit off if I miss a day. I try every morning to list three "grateful for" things that happened to me the day before. It's cool because your brain begins scanning for and reliving only the happy stuff in your yesterday. I should say that I'm grateful for you, Mr. Achor. Your idea really helps me focus on what's important: good gets the ink, bad doesn't get a second thought.

OCTOBER 20

The best portion of your life will be the
small, nameless moments you spend
smiling with someone who matters to you.
— RITU GHATOUREY

One morning, when I laid Haley down on
the bed, we locked eyes. *Bam!* I don't know,
there was just something about the moment
that was unbelievable. I was overcome by
emotion . . . by our connection . . . by those
beautiful brown eyes. I started crying, tears
streaming down my cheeks. That's when my
sweet one-year-old reached up for me and
said, "Wet, Mama." I can still see and hear
her doing it. All I could think was, *Oh my
God, this child sees everything and feels
everything.* Our little thirty-second exchange
— that small, nameless moment — is tucked
away in my memory, picture perfect.

Life shrinks or expands in proportion to one's courage.

— Anaïs Nin

Sponsored by Spanx.

I'd rather learn to dance in the rain than worry if I have an umbrella for the rest of my life.

— Nikki Rowe

I'd totally agree with this . . . if I didn't have weather-sensitive hair.

Visualize your highest self. Start showing
up as her.

When I interviewed Tyler Perry on my
Sirius radio show, he shared the story of
how he not only visualized his future, he
lived it . . . sort of. Growing up extremely
poor in New Orleans, Tyler said that as a
teenager he would look up homes for sale
in beautiful neighborhoods and walk
through the open houses. He wanted to see
where he would live one day. The now-
multimillionaire would also visit car dealer-
ships and sit in the front seat of fancy rides
he would drive someday. What can my life
look like? I suppose that's called daydream-
ing, but Tyler not only had a dream, he cast
himself in the movie version.

OCTOBER 24

Parenting is yelling, "You just had a snack!" over and over until you give in and throw them another snack.

— @loud_momma

Um, exactly. So does this fall into the category of Pick Your Battles or You Stink as a Parent?

OCTOBER 25

People start to heal the moment they feel heard.
                                        — Cheryl Richardson

Because there's nothing worse than feeling like you have no voice. Except feeling like you do but no one's listening.

OCTOBER 26

Almost everything will work again if you unplug it for a few minutes . . . including you.

— Anne Lamott

Jenna Bush Hager and I once agreed to stay off social media for two weeks. We'd both proclaimed we were "sick of it" and admitted our own roles in dropping down useless rabbit holes, wasting time. My habit was to pop on technology when I was in traffic or waiting at appointments. So instead, I downloaded a few books. I gazed out the window in cars. "Look, it's snowing," I'd proudly point out. I called my mom . . . a lot. She eventually began answering with, "Why are you calling again?" She really thought something was wrong or weird or both. After two weeks, Jenna and I resumed our relationships with Twitter and Instagram. I must admit the break made me realize I do feel better when I don't let technology own me. That said, the other day I started reading an article, browsed the comments, tapped on a profile photo, and ended up scrolling through images of people barbecuing hamburgers. #$@&!

OCTOBER 27

Eventually all things fall into place. Until
then, laugh at the confusion, live for the
moments, and know everything happens
for a reason.
— ALBERT SCHWEITZER

I heard Haley Joy before I saw her: a little
cry. Then double doors opened and a
woman walked out cradling a baby. I
couldn't breathe and it seemed like everything was happening in slow motion. She
said, "Here's your daughter." Just like that.
And then *my daughter,* a tiny warm bundle,
was in my arms. Never in my life had I
experienced the emotions surging through
me! Haley looked beautiful; she looked like
she was mine, calm and content. In that
magical moment, everything about me,
about my life, changed. I couldn't believe
that a door I had thought was closed had
opened . . . and she had come through it.

In the days ahead, when I finally caught my breath, I shared the news . . . and my immense wonder. "I'm fifty-two and I have a baby." One friend offered, "That little baby is right on time." Was she ever! I've never been more ready for anything in my life, sweet girl.

Good things happen in your life when you surround yourself with positive people.

— Roy Bennett

I definitely believe that a positive posse is key. Good attitudes are contagious!

The book we really needed was *What to Expect 17 Years After You Were Expecting.*

Funny, but ouch. My daughters are still in the single digits, but I have many friends navigating the parenting journey with teenagers. From what I hear about how uncool Mom becomes, there are some heart-tugging challenges ahead. Still, I can't wait for all of it!

OCTOBER 30

The bad news is time flies. The good news
is you're the pilot.

— Michael Altshuler

Are we? Sometimes it doesn't feel like we're
in control. Maybe it's better to say we're
the copilots.

October 31

Sticky fingers, tired feet; one last house, trick or treat!

— Rusty Fischer

When Haley was nearly two years old, she got a taste of Halloween New York City style. Because residential areas aren't an easy walk away, we city people hit up our favorite neighborhood haunts for candy. The people-watching is so much fun! Because Haley loves bees — the ones she sees in books — I dressed her in a cute bumblebee costume. I wore a matching bee outfit, my mom rocked a striped shirt with a bee mask, and Joel killed it in a T-shirt that read: "I just wanna hang with my bees." C'mon! Our family buzzed in and out of Duane Reade, Neet Cleaners, and the City Diner, with Haley attempting "Trick or treat!" and "Thank you." This Halloween, we'll add little Hope to the fun. Maybe big sis will show her all she's learned about celebrating Halloween in the Big Carmel Apple.

NOVEMBER 1

Falling down is an accident, staying down is a choice.
— Rosemary Nonny Knight

If you're down, try to at least get to your knees. Then pray for the strength to stand up again.

The reason we struggle with insecurity: we're comparing our behind-the-scenes to everyone else's highlight reel.

— Steven Furtick

In 2007, Harriet Selwyn was asking me to show her something that had only been seen by doctors and nurses. "Let me see it," she said. My friend Jen's aunt Harriet wanted to check out my breast, mangled from post-cancer surgery. *No way,* I thought. Embarrassment had joined shock and fear in my cancer journey. How would I ever let anyone see my body? During her forties, Harriet had not only had a mastectomy, she'd posed topless baring both breasts — one full, one missing — in a group photo for a book celebrating cancer survivors. Now, before I knew what was happening, Harriet was lifting her shirt, exposing one flat breast with no nipple. "So what," she said, referring to her chest. "So. What." *Hmm,* I thought. I slowly pulled up my shirt and watched Harriet's eyes. "Good surgery," she said. I let out a long, deep breath and covered back up. In a matter of seconds, Harriet had become my "first," with zero drama for either of us. Sometimes we need help revealing our insecurities, don't we? If you show me yours, I'll show you mine.

NOVEMBER 3

Everything in life is easier when you don't concern yourself with what everyone else is doing.

Quite a challenge in this age of 24/7 access to what everyone else is doing! Still, it's a good reminder to take a break from technology once in a while.

November 4

Notice the people who are happy for your happiness, and sad for your sadness. They're the ones who deserve special places in your heart.

What a treasure it is to have people in your life who are *truly* happy for you when good things happen. Mine: Hala, Adel, Karen, Janie, Jen, my mom. Check your list . . . all you really need is one.

November 5

Character — the willingness to accept responsibility for one's own life — is the source from which self-respect springs.

— Joan Didion

Actress Ellie Kemper is the first to admit she can easily wallow in self-pity when something negative happens, and that's why she loves this quote. "I can't control that my series [*Unbreakable Kimmy Schmidt*] ended, but I *can* control how I react to it," she says, "and that's where the wisdom lies." Ellie admits it's not always easy to take personal responsibility, but in the end, that's what builds character. "Blaming external stuff is wrong. You make the bed that you're going to lie down in, so make it something you're proud of and that you respect. You'll be a much happier person." At a time when so many people crave "likes" and search for social validation, Ellie finds the quote even more powerful. "This is saying, 'No, no, no . . . you have to like yourself.' "

NOVEMBER 6

Storms make trees take deeper roots.
— DOLLY PARTON

Whatever Dolly is singing or writing about, I'm in. She is one of the most sincere, funny, talented people I've ever met. I will *never* forget the moment when one of Dolly's biggest fans had the chance to meet her in person. Megan Stackhouse, who heads up the public relations department for *Today,* has met every superstar celebrity who's been booked on the show. From Beyoncé to Tom Hanks, Megan's shaken their hand. That's why I was so shocked by what unfolded when Dolly was on set one morning. Because I knew Megan loved Dolly, I called her over during a commercial break to meet her. She resisted! I couldn't believe it. I had to practically drag her over. When she finally stood in front of Dolly, she started to cry. Dolly gently asked, "Are you okay?" Confused but ever so genuine, Dolly opened her arms and Megan fell into them. Through tears, she said, "You have no idea, but you practically raised me, Dolly." It was so beautiful . . . Dolly and the young girl who finally had the chance to say thank you.

NOVEMBER 7

Do something today that your future self
will thank you for.
> — Sean Patrick Flanery

Yeah. Pay it forward, today's self.

If you don't like something change it; if you
can't change it, change the way you think
about it.

— Mary Engelbreit

To me, this quote is awesome because it's
doable. Reprogramming the way we view a
challenge may be difficult, but it can be
done! We have control over our thoughts, so
why not make them work *for* us, not against
us?

NOVEMBER 9

Be with someone who always wants to know how your day was.

And who's willing to listen to you unpack the good, the bad, and the ugly.

It's OK if you fall down and lose your spark. Just make sure that when you get back up, you rise as the whole damn fire.
— Colette Werden

When I was on the high school track team, I'll never forget the meet where my friend Wendy had a rough go of it. She was a hurdler and we were cheering her on from the sidelines at the start of her event. As the race unfolded, Wendy glided along, clearing every hurdle. Then, with the foot of her trail leg, she clipped a hurdle and stumbled. We kept on yelling. When she clipped another and tripped again, the team got nervous. It seemed things couldn't get much worse. But they did. Wendy's foot hit one of the last hurdles and she face-planted. We all gasped as she lay on the track, devastated and hurting. Slowly, Wendy got herself up off the ground, wiped off the dust, and finished the race. Every athlete at the competition that day clapped for her. I'll never forget our coach's speech to us after the meet. He said, "If you got a medal this afternoon, you earned it. But here's the real winner today," and he pointed at our scraped-up teammate. "It's Wendy," he said.

NOVEMBER 11

Home of the free because of the brave.

On a Facebook page called Love What Matters, there's a story about a little girl who was walking through the grocery store wearing oversized cowboy boots. A woman in the store noticed and approached the girl's mother in the checkout line to say how cute her daughter looked. The girl grinned and said, "The boots are my daddy's, and today would have been his birthday, but he died in Afghanistan." Her mom explained that she let her daughter wear the boots to make her feel a little better. A man in line who overheard the story took a cupcake from the batch he was buying and gave it to the little girl. "We are going to celebrate your dad's birthday today," he said. How absolutely beautiful. Maybe take a look at the photo of that little girl in the boots today.

We thank you, our dear veterans, and all who continue to serve. We love you.

November 12

It's okay to be scared. Being scared
means you're about to do something
really, really brave.
— MANDY HALE

It's interesting how fear and anxiety and
excitement are cousins. They're related but
so different in how they motivate us. I suppose sometimes we just have to feel afraid
and still see a green — not red — light.

NOVEMBER 13

Friday the 13th is still better than Monday the whatever.

Sunday night just yelled, "Darn right!"

NOVEMBER 14

Do more of what makes you happy.

STEP 1: Figure out what makes you happy.
STEP 2: Do more of it!

November 15

Don't compare your life to others'. There's no comparison between the sun and the moon. They shine when it's their time.

Comparing is exhauuuusting, too.

November 16

Don't be so hard on yourself. The mom in E.T. had an alien life form living in her house for days and she never even noticed.

Exactly. We good!

November 17

It's one of the greatest gifts you can give yourself, to forgive. Forgive everybody.
— Maya Angelou

At first glance, forgiveness seems like you're giving someone else a pass — someone who's hurt or wronged you. But the quote gets it right, I think. As hard as it can be sometimes, forgiveness is a gift we can give *ourselves*. "I forgive you" is a graceful way of saying, "I'm taking back my peace of mind."

NOVEMBER 18

Impossible odds set the stage for amazing miracles.

On February 7, 2010, I was lucky enough to be one of the thousands of people in Miami's Sun Life Stadium to watch the New Orleans Saints beat the Indianapolis Colts in Super Bowl XLIV. I was covering the game for *Today* as a biased correspondent, decked out in my beloved black and gold. When I arrived, South Beach felt like Bourbon Street, swarming with fellow Saints fans. Due to decades of losses, the Saints were known as the Ain'ts, but now . . . here they were at the big dance. Fans were a collective nervous wreck throughout the game. Only when the clock showed double zeros did Saints fans explode, finally believing their eyes and the 31–17 win on the scoreboard. When my crew and I scrambled onto the field, I was overwhelmed, smack-dab in the middle of history. I could see Drew Brees tearing up, sharing the moment with his baby, Baylen, in his arms. I could feel New Orleans healing, embracing a win for their team and their city, ravaged five years earlier by Hurricane Katrina. *Wow.* Impossible odds had indeed set the stage for an amazing miracle.

NOVEMBER 19

Faith is one foot on the ground, one foot in the air, and a queasy feeling in the stomach.

— Mother Angelica

My best friend, Karen, is one of the strongest people I know, and it's her deep sense of faith that grounds and sustains her. Ever since I've known her, and especially during a devastating family journey through her husband's cancer — when she not only endured her own sorrow but witnessed their young daughter, Catherine, lose her father — Karen's belief in God has never wavered. "Next to love, faith is the greatest gift," Karen says. "It endures all and propels us forward no matter the obstacle in our path. Faith reminds us that no matter what, with God, everything will be okay." May God continue to bless you, Karen and Catherine, and John up in heaven.

Impossible is just an opinion.
— Paulo Coelho

I've seen motivational articles that change the word "Impossible" to "I'm possible." Love that.

NOVEMBER 21

A moment of patience in a moment of anger saves you a thousand moments of regret.

And those thousand moments are the *worst,* aren't they?! Regret is so stubborn. I still think about something I didn't do ten years ago. One morning in New York, I was walking down Broadway in a rush to get to work. I passed a mother holding a baby and she said she needed help. What I heard was, "I need money." Having just been to the bank, I gave her what I had on me. "I don't want money," she said. "We need a place to stay." I apologized and told her I hoped the money would help, leaving her behind as I headed for 30 Rock. To this day, I can picture her eyes . . . pleading. She's still on my mind. I hope someone helped her in a real way. It should have been me.

Dear God, I wanna take a minute, not to ask for anything from you, but simply to say thank you for all I have.

On this day, God gave my family Adel. To me, my younger brother is gold. He's patient, humble, funny, calm, and ever so generous. For my first job out of college, I was required to have a car. The Greenville, Mississippi, television market was so small that reporters had to provide their own news vehicles. I was flat broke, and Adel went with me to the car lot to look for a clunker. The car dealer would not let me buy a car without putting money down, so I was in a pickle. Guess who wrote a check for a thousand dollars? Yep, Adel. He'd worked all summer long at Popeyes Louisiana Kitchen and saved every dime. Without blinking, Adel whipped out his checkbook and spent his entire summer salary . . . on

me. Dear God, I want to take a minute to
say thank you for Adel, and for all of my
many blessings.

Some people come into our lives and quickly go. Some stay for a while and leave footprints on our heart, and we are never, ever the same.

— Flavia Weedn

Some tread lightly and others stomp around, but all footprints are important. They teach us things.

November 24

Sometimes you win, sometimes you
learn.
— JOHN C. MAXWELL

This is such a great win-win!

I am not a "glass half full" type of person. I am a "where did I put my glass?" kind of person.

I am definitely both of those types!

NOVEMBER 26

Gratitude is not only the greatest of virtues,
but the parent of all the others.
>   — Marcus Tullius Cicero

One of the reasons I love Thanksgiving is
that gratitude is always the main dish.
(Another reason is Colleen's amazing
mashed potatoes!) A grateful heart certainly
serves us well all year round, too.

Miracles start to happen when you give as much energy to your dreams as you do to your fears.

— Richard Wilkins

It truly was a miracle when all four judges flipped their chairs around for the Winos on season 14 of *The Voice.* Kathie Lee and I showed up for the blind auditions and chose James Taylor's "You've Got a Friend" for our duet. Obviously, Kathie Lee can sing; obviously, I cannot. When Kris Jenner (part of our behind-the-scenes support group) heard me start singing, she said, "Oh, Hoda, God bless you." My heart was pounding and I was terrified, but I tried to sell the song with swaying arm movements and grunts. Finally, Kelly Clarkson, Alicia Keys, Blake Shelton, and Adam Levine all turned around! I was so grateful for the end of that song and for Kathie Lee. Blake said it best:

"Hoda, Kathie Lee saved your a— on that one."

Never worry about numbers. Help one person at a time, and always start with the person nearest you.
— Saint Teresa of Calcutta

Many Sundays I'm sitting atop a bike in spin class, my fellow riders and me letting the music soak into our soul as we churn through the miles in the opposite direction of our troubles. One morning, my favorite instructor, Sue Molnar, played the version of the song "Hallelujah" sung by its writer, Leonard Cohen. As I listened to the lyrics about holy things and broken things, my emotional walls began to crumble. But I held it together and pedaled harder . . . until I noticed a rider dismounting his bike. A man began to walk around the room, hugging each person. He was moved by the song, wanted to reach out, and everyone let him. One by one, riders slowed their pumping knees to share a moment with him. When he wrapped his arms around me, I cried. All of the mental crap I'd brought in with me trickled down my face. How about that guy? He was fearless, rejection be damned. Of everything I did that weekend, those four minutes and thirty-nine seconds of "Hallelujah" were the best.

NOVEMBER 29

Sometimes you find yourself in the middle
of nowhere, and sometimes in the middle
of nowhere you find yourself.

I think this is one of the reasons so many
people love to hike and camp and wander. I
like to be smack-dab in the middle of a
sunny beach somewhere.

Online shopping: Because it's frowned upon to be in a store with no bra, sweatpants, and a glass of wine.

Grab your glass and clickety-clack, friends!

December 1

In French you don't really say "I miss you." You say, "Tu me manques" which is closer to "You are missing from me."

This makes me picture someone creating a heart shape with both hands. The hole in the middle — "You are missing from me."

DECEMBER 2

You teach people how to treat you by what you allow, what you stop, and what you reinforce.

— Tony A. Gaskins Jr.

To figure this out early in life would be ideal, wouldn't it? Maybe it gets easier as we get older because we have more experience with relationships. Still, both personally and professionally, I think this concept — while spot-on — can be complex and takes practice to master.

DECEMBER 3

Simply let go of the illusion that it could have been any different.

— Jeff Foster

Perhaps it's self-preservation, but we all rewrite (or re-remember) history sometimes. But what would happen if we let go of how we wish things were and faced how they *really* are? Maybe we'd focus on doing our best right now, instead of pounding our heads against the past.

DECEMBER 4

Focus on the powerful, euphoric, magical, beautiful parts of life, and the universe will keep giving them to you.

And really, the journey is far more meaningful that way, isn't it?

DECEMBER 5

The way we spend our time defines who
we are.

— JONATHAN ESTRIN

I guess because every ticktock is so precious.
Consider that when we spend money, we
can make more. When we spend time, it's
gone forever.

DECEMBER 6

The thing about new beginnings is that they require something else to end.
— Blair Waldorf, *Gossip Girl*

Goodbyes can be very hard, but there's something pretty great about *finally* clearing the way for a fresh start.

DECEMBER 7

We can't help everyone, but everyone can help someone.
— Ronald Reagan

This reminds me of writer Anne Lamott's approach to tackling a big project. She tells the story of her brother's struggling with a homework assignment about birds. He'd had three months to write the paper, but of course he'd procrastinated, and now the report was due the next day. He was over-whelmed, frozen in uncertainty, and unsure where to start. Her father came to the rescue, encouraging her brother to take things one step at a time. "Bird by bird, buddy," he guided Anne's brother. "Just take it bird by bird."

Keep an eye out. *Someone* may need a little boost today.

DECEMBER 8

There is always something to be grateful for.

Sue is my favorite spinning instructor and I call her Soul Cycle Sue. In about 2017, she began a fight with cancer that I'm thankful to report she's winning. I'll never forget the day that she woke us all up — fired us up — with just a few words. There she was, bald and walking around the room, as we huffed and puffed and considered giving up for a nice long break. Then she said it: "What I wouldn't do," she boomed over her headset, "to be on one of those bikes right now." Woooooooooooooow. Instantly, pedals began to spin at double speed. You'd have thought it was raining Red Bull. Riders stood up and pumped like crazy. Sue had dropped a perspective bomb and, boy, did we respond. Today — and every day — we can be grateful for something.

December 9

Don't wait for everything to be perfect
before you decide to enjoy your life.
— Joyce Meyer

When I see pairs of shoes — from small to
large — cluttering the front hall of my
apartment, it's perfectly imperfect. They
mean that a bunch of my favorite people
are visiting.

DECEMBER 10

Be an encourager. The world has plenty of critics already.

— Dave Willis

Pom-poms up and shakin', y'all!

DECEMBER 11

The hardest thing in the world is to simplify
your life. It's easy to make it complex.
— Yvon Chouinard

Yup. Right now on my phone I have 11,942
unread emails, 176 unread texts, 91 unheard
voicemails, 119 apps, 19,299 photos, and
countless songs. Today's my day to start
simplifying! (Delete, delete, delete . . .) How
about you?

December 12

Imagine all the things we could be if we weren't controlled by insecurity.

> — Bridgett Devoue

I've heard Kathie Lee say it often: "I don't give a rip." Usually, that phrase pops up when she's forging ahead, being herself, making a decision to slough off insecurity and boldly go where her heart and mind lead her. An intern at NBC once told me that his mother is inspired by Kathie Lee's confidence. If she's headed into a situation where she needs a boost of self-assurance, his mom will say, "I've got to get my Kathie Lee on." Yes! Need to get *your* Kathie Lee on today?

December 13

Whenever you are creating beauty
around you, you are restoring your own
soul.

— ALICE WALKER

The last twenty minutes of my Sirius radio
show one Monday turned out to be the
best. I was interviewing a photographer
about his book featuring abused dogs
adopted into loving homes. On air, Richard
Phibbs shared with me that during his thirties — when photography was merely a
hobby — several crushing personal challenges led him into therapy. During one ses-
sion, the therapist said, "You know, Richard, creativity can be healing. The way
you're going to save yourself is to put
something beautiful out into the world."

Skeptical but curious, Richard picked up
his camera and began snapping portraits of
his friends. Before long, his photos were

selected for a Ralph Lauren advertisement campaign. Richard remembers leaving work that day thinking, *What just happened?* He went on to have a successful career shooting fashion and capturing the likes of Meryl Streep, Jay Z, and Hillary Clinton. (And happy dogs.) The "something beautiful" Richard put out into the airwaves that day inspired me to post Alice Walker's quote.

DECEMBER 14

Slow down. Happiness is trying to catch you.

At least give it a fighting chance to tackle you, tickle you, and stay for a while.

DECEMBER 15

Just being there is ninety-nine percent of what matters when your world falls apart.
— Holly Goldberg Sloan

Oh dear. There are so many among us who struggle mightily each day to show up. If this is you, we respect your strength.

DECEMBER 16

Freedom lies across the field of the difficult conversation. And the more difficult the conversation, the greater the freedom.
— Shonda Rhimes

Ugh! We don't want to have "the talk," but *not* having it is unsettling, too. No one wants to be hurt or disappointed or rejected, but serenity one-ups all of those, doesn't it?

DECEMBER 17

The best and most beautiful things in the world cannot be seen or even touched, but just felt in the heart.

— Helen Keller

Music is surely one of these beautiful things.

DECEMBER 18

Making the decision to have a child is momentous. It is to decide forever to have your heart go walking around outside your body.

— Elizabeth Stone

As I eased into my fifties, little signals kept urging me to speak out loud about my desire to have children. For so long, I'd only been talking to myself. *Am I too old? Can my busy life support such an important role as Mommy?* And then I read that Sandra Bullock had adopted her kids later in life. After an energizing phone call with Sandy, my heart said, *Why not me?* Then, while covering the Summer Olympics in Rio de Janeiro, I saw a heart-wrenching photo of a small boy coated with ashes and dried blood after an airstrike in Syria. *There are so many children who need help,* I thought. And there was nothing I wanted more than to be a mom. When I flew home, I was finally ready to share my desire aloud . . . to Joel. "You don't have to tell me right now — take a minute — but I'd like to explore the possibility of adopting a baby with you." There. I'd put it out into the world. Without skipping a beat, Joel said, "I don't need a minute. Let's do it." While we waited, I posted this quote. A few weeks later, our baby arrived.

DECEMBER 19

Chase grace.

One of the most memorable moments of the 2016 Summer Olympics Games in Rio de Janeiro unfolded during the women's 5,000 meter heat. If I recall correctly, I was watching the race inside the International Broadcast Centre, a temporary setup for broadcasters around the world. Four laps from the finish, New Zealand runner Nikki Hamblin and United States runner Abbey D'Agostino collided, falling to the ground in a scrum of tightly packed bodies. What happened next was unforgettable. In an act of true grace, D'Agostino helped up her competitor and began to run with her, limping on her injured leg. But, in severe pain, Hamblin couldn't continue, so D'Agostino stayed with her, hugging and supporting a person she'd never met. Millions of us were moved by such a selfless gesture. "When I look back on Rio 2016," said a grateful Hamblin, "I'm not going to remember where I finished, I'm not going to remember my time . . . but I'll always remember that moment."

DECEMBER 20

Sometimes your heart needs more time
to accept what your mind already knows.

Okay, but the amount of time we wait
between those emotions is never the same.
Some pain is so deep that it's gonna take a
while.

I saw that.

— God

My other favorite: "Jesus is coming. Look busy."

The secret of patience is to do something else in the meantime.

— Croft M. Pentz

I think this is one of the reasons we spend so much time with technology, don't you? Whether it's right or wrong, our screens are the easy go-to when we're feeling antsy or anxious. I'll bet knitters are patient people . . .

DECEMBER 23

It's okay to have a meltdown. Just don't
unpack and live there.

Little kids are the best at this. I'm always
amazed at how quickly Haley moves on, giggling with meltdown tears still trickling
down her face.

December 24

'Twas the night before Christmas, when all through the house, not a creature was stirring, not even a mouse.
— Clement Clarke Moore,
A Visit from St. Nicholas

I love this sweet image. I also love the other story: parents swearing at assembly instructions and shaking the already-wrapped gifts, thinking, *Which kid is this one for again?* The chaos and the celebration. It's all so awesome!

December 25

Be the reason someone believes in the goodness of people.

— Karen Salmansohn

At holiday time, letters addressed to the North Pole are sometimes read by postal workers before they reach Santa Claus. During Christmas of 2016, *Today* show producer Robin Sindler and I teamed up on a project to surprise underprivileged kids with the requests they'd made to Santa in writing: "I just need some clothes, warm sweaters." Or, "I'm 7 and live with my mom and three brothers. Just give us what you think we deserve." Fourth graders from the Brooklyn YMCA served as our elves, helping to read the letters and wrap gifts. During the project, I noticed a girl reading a particularly moving note, elf ears atop her head. When I asked how she was doing, she said, "I'm happy we're getting them things, but I feel sad. I don't even know if we should have Christmas." *Gulp.* What a big heart in that little girl. The day was such a great reminder for us all that it is indeed better to give than to receive.

DECEMBER 26

Sometimes you have to surrender before
you win.
— GREGORY DAVID ROBERTS

It's a relief sometimes, isn't it, to let go? To
surrender. Sometimes we need a long break,
sometimes we just need a new day. (Especially this time of year . . .)

DECEMBER 27

Embrace the chaos and choose joy.

My countertops are sticky, the floor is covered with kid stuff, and I'm smiling ear to ear.

DECEMBER 28

Coincidence is God's way of remaining anonymous.

Some people call coincidences God winks. I like this take on them, too.

DECEMBER 29

Smiling does not necessarily mean you're happy. Sometimes it just means you're strong.

I love this. There's so much behind a smile, and sometimes it's just sheer will.

DECEMBER 30

Be good to people.

In the Denver airport one morning, a hooded T-shirt in a kiosk caught my eye. It featured this phrase on the front. What a find! I had to have it, a cozy billboard for such a simple yet precious message.

DECEMBER 31

Tomorrow is the first blank page of a 365-page book. Write a good one.

— Brad Paisley

The anticipation of a brand-new start really puts the sparkle in New Year's Eve! Still, one year it fizzled for my sister, Hala, and me hours before the big countdown. She was visiting me in New Orleans and our plan was set for a festive night out to celebrate. Dressed to the nines, we looked at each other right before heading out the door and I said, "Wanna stay home instead?" Hala laughed and agreed immediately! We traded our party clothes for pajamas and spent an awesome evening binge-watching movies and eating popcorn. And you know what? We still talk about how much fun we had that night.

Aren't quotes the best?

Honestly, I couldn't wait to share this book with you. While I love our connection on Instagram, there's just something so special about this keepsake, tuck-in-your-tote format. In one cozy bundling of quotes and notes, I get to connect with you — and only you — one page at a time.

In March 2019, I couldn't help but notice something very cool happening when I began a speaking tour for my second children's book. During that week, the universe seemed to be raising its hand, requesting this book. I couldn't believe it! People at events would ask me, "What's your favorite quote that you've posted?" Or they'd hand me a piece of paper and say, "Look! I've written down quotes that mean the most to me." At every single appearance I made — and even on the plaza at work — people wanted to share their deep feelings about quotes. Your endless enthusiasm gave me goose bumps! Even though this idea was already in motion, the buzz about the power of words confirmed to me that a book would be impactful. So many people seemed ready to hold the words in their hands, not just scroll through them on a screen. The book's title makes me happy, too, because it was inspired by so many of you who posted *I really needed this today* in the comment section alongside a quote. Thank you!

Now that you've read the book, I'm curious about how you engaged with it. Did you soak up one quote per day, or did you read for a half hour at a time? Maybe you were motivated to take a chance, a second look, or a slow, deep breath. Way to go! After all, the quote didn't do the work; you did. May your growth or glowing sense of optimism inspire others to take their own journey through these pages. In fact, I hope you'll consider lending the book to someone else.

I'll close for now with my thanks to you for supporting *I Really Needed This Today.* Together we have celebrated the magic of connection — we need each other, we know each other, we are each other.

Hoda xo

ACKNOWLEDGMENTS

I can't say enough to all of you who have connected with the many quotes I've shared over the years. That you are out there, open to the power of words, is meaningful to me. The way you share quotes with the people you love is endearing, too. We truly need each other to navigate life and its daily challenges — thank you.

And to everyone who strings words together in a way that makes us want to better something about ourselves, soothe others, or change the world, we are forever grateful.

There is no book without you, Cait Hoyt. Besides being my CAA book agent extraordinaire, you're just a lovely human being with a heart of gold. You don't just feel things deeply, you're the deep thinker who came up with the idea for this book. You not only saw the opportunity, you made us all believe in it with your heartfelt pitch: it will help people.

That's what I love, too, about the team at Penguin Random House — you all were motivated by what this book could do: inspire, comfort, and entertain readers. Executive editor Michelle Howry, you just kept saying yes, even when that meant throwing an XL monkey wrench into designs and deadlines. Thanks for juggling, cheerleading, and expertly guiding us to the finish line. Many thanks to the following for your endless work and creativity: Alexis Welby, Ashley McClay, Christine Ball, Sally Kim, and Ivan Held. To the diligent sales team, your enthusiasm is bananas and I love that.

And finally, to my dear and incredibly talented friend Janie — you don't know how good you are. You do things with words that I didn't know were possible. I'm in awe of your talent. The fact that you hate reading this praise about you makes me love you even more.

ABOUT THE AUTHOR

Hoda Kotb was named co-host of the fourth hour of *Today* in 2007 and co-anchor of the flagship hour in 2018. She has also been a *Dateline NBC* correspondent since 1998 and is a *New York Times* bestselling author for her books *Hoda* and *Ten Years Later,* as well as for her two children's books, *I've Loved You Since Forever* and *You Are My Happy.* The four-time Emmy winner has also been honored multiple times with the Alliance for Women in Media's Gracie Award (most recently in 2019), as well as with the 2006 Peabody Award and the 2002 Edward R. Murrow Award. She resides in New York City with her partner, Joel, and her daughters, Haley and Hope.

The employees of Thorndike Press hope you have enjoyed this Large Print book. All our Thorndike, Wheeler, and Kennebec Large Print titles are designed for easy reading, and all our books are made to last. Other Thorndike Press Large Print books are available at your library, through selected bookstores, or directly from us.

For information about titles, please call:
(800) 223-1244

or visit our website at:
gale.com/thorndike

To share your comments, please write:

Publisher
Thorndike Press
10 Water St., Suite 310
Waterville, ME 04901